Contents

Preface

Whether you are a novice teacher or one with many years of experience, I think it is fair to say that teaching math can often prove challenging and sometimes even overwhelming. This isn't helped by the fact that, over the last number of years, there has been an increased focus placed on curriculum expectations in mathematics. And, while this is a good thing, it can add to the stress level of the teacher.

I think of some of the information that I was inundated with when teaching mathematics:

- A math curriculum consisting of mathematical concepts compartmentalized into strands. Within this curriculum, a provided list of outcomes and associated processes that students need to master by the end of the school year.
- A year plan that outlines when each outcome should be addressed and how much time is to be spent on each outcome.
- The underpinning notion that all students should be problem solvers.
- The expectation that classroom experiences be relevant. Students should be assigned rich and meaningful tasks that connect to their experiences.
- The expectation that students be provided a range of opportunities to explore and apply mathematical concepts.
- The requirement that students be provided with choice, in both the problems they solve and how they work through such problems.
- There should be a balance of whole-group, small-group, and individual activities.
- The need to have evidence of student learning in more than one context.
- Meeting the learning needs of all students in the classroom through thoughtful differentiated instruction.

The above list is not exhaustive, but it does paint a picture of the complexity, or messiness (as I am referring to it as in this book), associated with teaching mathematics. Put all these demands together and it can easily be seen that teaching math can be daunting, even for the best of us. For this reason, I firmly believe that teachers are, and have always been, burning the candle at both ends and working at an unsustainable rate.

During my time as a teacher, coach, consultant, leader, and teaching administrator, I have observed many teachers struggling to work through the messiness. And, while teachers spend countless hours trying to navigate this messiness, they are still left frustrated with the outcome, often sharing that their instructional goals are not being met. To meet the numerous demands placed on teachers, educational authorities have put many initiatives forward. Sadly, these initiatives only seem to add to the workload of teachers as they are often in conflict with one another or, at the very least, do not take the other into consideration.

Over time (whether it was working in my own classroom or during conversations and collaborations with other teachers, schools, and/or associations), I have identified a framework that removes the messiness associated with teaching mathematics. Teachers do not have to work with conflicting initiatives; instead, they can put the puzzle pieces together to address the many learning needs of their students in a way that is effective, yet manageable and sustainable.

This framework is made of three parts: **key concepts**, **problem types**, and **teacher moves**.

The **first component** of the framework is identifying **key concepts** in math. When teachers can identify key math concepts, they not only strengthen their understanding of high-leverage math concepts, but they can also approach instruction from a value-added perspective that will support all students in learning. Applying a key-concept approach to mathematics enables both teacher and students to strengthen the interconnectedness of mathematical concepts.

The **second component** within the framework is a teacher's toolbox of **problem types**. The power of this toolbox lies in the range of problems it contains. When providing students with a range of problems, the teacher is better able to address the vast learning needs in the classroom. A diverse toolbox can allow for whole-group, small-group, and/or individual tasks, provide classroom experiences that are rich and meaningful, and promote problem solving through offering choice to students in exploring and applying mathematical concepts.

The **third component** within the framework is referred to as **teacher moves**. Teacher moves is a concept that focuses on making instructional decisions based on student responses. By offering a range of problems, teachers are provided greater opportunities to get a more detailed snapshot of student learning. Student responses serve as evidence of learning and are used by the teacher as they analyze them against the common misconceptions associated with key mathematical concepts (referred to as *look fors*). One significant aspect when considering teacher moves is anticipation. It is important for the teacher to anticipate what they may see within student work. This anticipation is greatly aided by having a good understanding of key concepts, *look fors*, and common misconceptions. When anticipating possible student responses, teachers can craft questions that will elicit misconceptions. This type of preparedness can help teachers respond more intuitively to any misconceptions a student may have during an interaction.

This **three-part framework** (key concepts, problem types, and teacher moves) is a game-changer for teachers. I have had the privilege to see it work in my own single and combined-grade classrooms, as well as in different grade levels in other schools within Canada and the United States. My goal is to share it with all teachers as it consists of subtle changes to instruction that yield significant increases in student achievement.

I want more for teachers and their students. I want teachers to see an increase in student achievement that they are looking for. I want to contribute what I can to assisting teachers in achieving their instructional goals. I want to address how overwhelmed teachers are feeling so that they not only understand the mathematics they are teaching but also have an approach to instruction that meets the many demands of their classroom.

Introduction

Consider your teaching assignment. Now, let's focus in on mathematics. When you begin to focus on math, what image, experience, concept, and/or instructional practice goes through your mind? I am guessing that it is not just one of these things, but many. In fact, it can feel like you are going down a rabbit hole when you start to consider the many factors associated with teaching math. And, for this reason, many consider mathematics to be messy. Whether it is the math concepts being explored, the instructional practices being considered, and/or the vast range of learning needs in the classroom; many educators quickly recognize that teaching math can be quite overwhelming. It is for this very reason that *Messing Around with Math* exists.

Let's burrow into some of the finer points in teaching mathematics. Read the following questions and consider your responses:

- Can you provide an overview of the mathematics that form the foundation for your grade level(s)?
- Can you identify the mathematical concepts within your grade level(s) that are key to student achievement?
- Can you identify the *look fors* that demonstrate student understanding of the key mathematical concepts?
- Can you identify possible misconceptions associated with key mathematical concepts?
- What is your comfort level with crafting questions to uncover student learning and to extend learning experiences?
- Are you providing a range of problems to your students so that they have a varied experience with the mathematical concept?
- Are the problems you assign students providing an opportunity for student choice (in terms of multiple points of entry and strategy selection)?
- Are the problems you assign students accounting for different lived experiences?
- Are the problems you assign students providing them with opportunities to problem solve? Or are they only for practice?

- Do you have access to problems that can be used at different points within the math lesson?
- Are the problems you assign students reflective of rich, meaningful tasks?
- Do you feel comfortable in crafting problems that can be used in the classroom?

If you are feeling as though these questions are complicated and that you are struggling to answer some or many of them, you are not alone. I ask these questions not to discourage you, but to highlight some of considerations that teachers must take into account when teaching mathematics. From a visual perspective, we have something like the following:

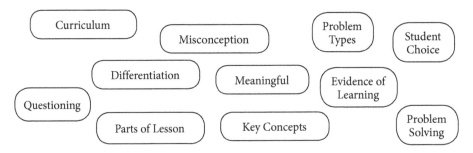

The visual above highlights how messy math can be. It is multifaceted when you consider the content, instructional approach, student learning needs, and how you want to integrate all of these into a learning experience that is relevant to students. As a way to address this messiness, let's consider it within a workable framework. To do this, we will use three main categories: key concepts, problem types, and teacher moves.

Three-Part Framework

Too often, professional learning resources are limited in scope. Teachers are either provided with a surface-level overview of a concept, a specific instructional strategy to implement, or a type of problem to introduce to the classroom. While there may be a blip in growth of student learning, the impact is not long-term. This short-term growth can be attributed to a teacher only addressing one part of the learning process (Costello, 2021).

The three-part framework considers three parts of the learning process: curriculum (key concepts), instruction (problem types), and assessment and student learning (teacher moves). When considering all three parts (as opposed to only focusing on a single part), we see teachers facilitating an environment where there are substantial gains in student learning over the long-term. It is the fitting together of these puzzle pieces that make this framework effective, manageable, and sustainable. When the pieces fit together, there is synergy and time is not wasted trying to align practices that don't correlate. It is a concise framework that takes into consideration things that matter.

This three-part framework is not meant to add more to a teacher's workload. Instead, it is intended to be used to identify the aspects of mathematics that yield the most value in terms of student learning, so that teachers can find an effective, yet manageable and sustainable way, to support their students in the complex setting of the classroom.

A visual representation of the three-part framework can be as follows:

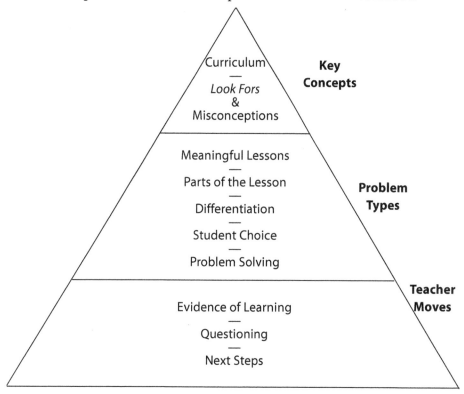

You may notice that aspects I referenced in the first visual are referenced in this second visual as well. The three-part framework (key concepts, problem types, and teacher moves) is a way to organize how we approach the messiness in mathematics. Each of the considerations that teachers must make when planning and teaching mathematics are still accounted for in the visual above. What the three-part framework provides is a way to remove the messiness while not losing out on the richness within the math lesson (content and instruction).

We still want students to be problem-solvers. We still want students to be engaged in productive struggle. When teachers can effectively identify key concepts and utilize a supply of multiple problem types, they'll have more opportunities to apply high-yield teacher moves that have significant impact on student achievement.

While these three parts of the framework are interwoven, it is important to take time to consider them individually so that we can take a deep dive into the approach.

Key Concepts

When given the curriculum for their grade level(s), many teachers quickly skim through the required four to six strands to get a sense of the number of outcomes and the range of concepts that are to be addressed during the year. It does not take long before teachers begin to stress over how to ensure students understand the many outcomes required and if they can apply concepts to solve assigned problems. However, during these initial and subsequent scans of the curriculum document, it becomes apparent that there are *some* curriculum outcomes that have more impact on student learning than others. These curriculum outcomes that are more significant than others are referred to as key concepts (Ainsworth, 2003).

To assist teachers in becoming comfortable with key concepts, I have grouped grades into a set of ranges. In Chapter 1, the following ranges are used:

- Kindergarten
- Grades 1–3 (Primary)
- Grades 4–6 (Elementary)

For each of the grade ranges listed above, I have highlighted key concepts and grouped them by type. Not only does this help teachers see common threads throughout the curriculum, but it also gives them a way to quickly sift through the book and find what they need (i.e., if you are working with fractions in Grade 5, you'll find all key concepts related to fractions grouped together).

Later in the book, I provide a brief overview of the foundational aspects of each key concept, then share associated problem types, teacher moves, possible *look fors* in regard to students demonstrating understanding, and common misconceptions found in student work. The intent is that this information will aid you, as the teacher, in strengthening your understanding of the key concepts and guide you in planning next steps for students.

Problem Types

It is important to take time to consider the problems we assign in the classroom. Where do you find the problem sets you assign? Are the problems you assign structured similarly? Why do you select the problems you assign? Do the problems you assign move learning forward, or are they busy work? Are the problems you assign helping students meet learning goals?

The problem types we use greatly impact the experience of students in the classroom. First, problems can either help or hinder a teacher in meeting the many learning needs of students. Whether the problem is open- or close-ended will influence whether students can enter the problem and/or reach a solution. Second, the problem can either engage or disengage students. If the problem is not relevant to students, they may have little motivation to work through to a solution. Third, if the problems are all similar in structure, they are not providing students with enough opportunities to problem solve. Instead, it is more reflective of practice because the novelty of the problem is lost.

It is through solving problems that students have the opportunity to apply their **mathematical understanding**. A carefully crafted problem will elicit student responses that will indicate to the teacher whether students understand a concept and can apply a strategy within a context. And, it is through solving problems that students have an opportunity to work through a task and demonstrate **social-emotional learning skills** during productive struggle.

Problems play a significant role in math instruction and learning. It is through problems that students encounter, explore, and apply math concepts. Therefore, we need to broaden the problems that we, as teachers, bring into the classroom. Students need experiences with two categories of problem types: **defined problems** and **ill-defined problems** (Costello, 2022).

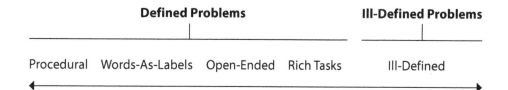

Defined Problems   **Ill-Defined Problems**

Procedural   Words-As-Labels   Open-Ended   Rich Tasks   Ill-Defined

Within these two categories of problems (defined and ill-defined), a continuum of problems is provided that all students should be experiencing in the classroom. However, many students are only being assigned defined problems. And, while there is some variance within defined problems, it is not enough. Only assigning students one category of problems would be like having students only read fictional texts. While a student could learn to read and read to learn using only fictional texts, their experience with literature would be severely limited.

As teachers, we must broaden the problem types we assign to include both defined and ill-defined types. By offering students both categories of problems, we are basing instruction and learning on the full continuum of problems available. And, in doing so, we provide students with a variety of experiences, broaden their perspective of key math concepts, strengthen their problem-solving skills, and move student work from *practicing* to *problem solving*.

To assist teachers in becoming comfortable with a variety of problem types, Chapter 2 consists of an overview of each problem category (defined and ill-defined) and highlights the different types of problems within each category. For each problem type, I've included alternate ways to structure and style them, shown how to craft opportunities for differentiation, and offered strategies to craft your own for each type. When exploring both the categories and types, core characteristics are highlighted and there are accompanying examples to assist in understanding them.

Teacher Moves

When working with mathematics, it is important for the teacher to recognize *look fors* in terms of student learning. *Look fors* are identifiable attributes displayed by students that demonstrate their understanding of the concept. They can be written, concrete (using manipulatives), oral, and/or pictorial.

When I talk with teachers, it does not take long to realize that they are the busiest people in the classroom. They are constantly observing students as they work, responding to their students' questions during independent practice, trying to craft problems on-the-spot to address a specific learning need, and thinking of ways to support students in moving forward. However, rarely have I met a teacher who is pleased with how well their students are progressing. Many teachers tell me that they are going above and beyond but are not seeing any positive impact in regard to student problem-solving and independence.

Teachers are doing a lot of work during the math block, and I want to help them see the impact of this work. To assist teachers in working smarter, not harder, I have highlighted some high-yield teacher moves that puts the onus on students to think mathematically and to work through the problem. Two such teacher moves are questioning and identifying next steps.

Later in this book I share questions that teachers can ask students (whether in whole-group, small-group, or individual settings) to aid students in developing their problem-solving abilities. In addition to sharing questions, I have identified next steps based on common misconceptions.

In This Book

Chapter 1 provides a list of key concepts for three grade ranges (Kindergarten, Grades 1 to 3, and Grades 4 to 6). The key concepts provided are meant to assist teachers in highlighting high-leverage curriculum outcomes and give them a list of outcomes to work and set learning goals with. They are grouped around central ideas so that teachers can easily sift through this book to identify problems that address a range of learning needs in the classroom.

Chapter 2 contains numerous examples of various problem types (from both defined and ill-defined problems). Each problem type is explored and comes with an overview of alternate structures and styles. There are also prompts so that teachers can craft their own problems to use in the classroom.

The remainder of the book is filled with a range of problem types that support student understanding of key math concepts. Chapter 3 covers Kindergarten, Chapter 4 covers Primary (Grades 1 to 3), and Chapter 5 covers Elementary (Grades 4 to 6).

When working with each key math concept and various problem types, I provide a brief overview of the key concepts, *look fors*, common misconceptions, and teacher moves. To offer further support, I make note of when problems could be positioned within the lesson (i.e., warm-up, independent practice, or consolidation).

To conclude the book, I have included a chapter outlining an approach for teachers to craft their own problems with—reflective of a variety of problem types. This chapter can be applied to any curricular strand that you are addressing.

Reproducibles that support students as they work through the various types of problems addressed within this book are included, beginning on page XX. The first two provide options for graphic organizers that can assist students in documenting their thinking as they problem-solve through defined problems. The third provides a visual of the mathematical modelling process that can be used to solve ill-defined problems. The last two reproducibles provide planning templates for teachers as they begin to work with key concepts.

From procedural problems, word problems, open-ended, rich tasks, to real-world math problems, *Messing Around with Math* provides you with a toolbox that will help you address the complex learning needs of your students. The problems found in this book can be used at any point in the lesson: whole-group teaching, guided small-group instruction, or independent practice. This resource will also help teachers develop their skills in crafting rich, meaningful, and engaging lessons. Instead of endless searching for the 'right' problem for your students, you will have a one-stop shop.

Messing Around with Math is a book that does not need to be read from start to finish. Instead, it is a book that can come out at any point in the school year and one that will probably remain on your desk as you progress throughout. Whether it is when you have questions about a key concept, need a variety of problems for any part of the math lesson, and/or are pondering possible teacher moves to assist students in taking next steps in their learning; you can rely on this instructional book to be a useful resource in helping you plan, teach, and assess student learning. It is a book that assists with both math content and instruction. Use it when you need it.

1

Redefining Problems

Key concepts are core curriculum outcomes that help with learning other outcomes more efficiently and effectively (Ainsworth, 2003). They form the basis for further learning, whether that learning takes place during the current school year or in subsequent years (Costello, 2021). For a curriculum outcome to be identified as a key concept, one or more of the following criteria must be met (Ainsworth, 2003):

- **Leverage**: Curriculum outcome(s) that focus on knowledge and skills used in multiple academic disciplines.
- **Endurance**: Outcomes and standards that focus on knowledge and skills that will be relevant throughout a student's lifetime.
- **Essentiality**: Outcomes and standards that focus on the knowledge and skills necessary for students to succeed in the next grade level.

Many curriculum outcomes selected as key concepts typically address two or three of the criteria above. Consider the following example of a key concept:

*Imagine you are an upper-elementary math teacher. One curriculum outcome would be working with percentages, whether it is ordering, comparing, or converting to decimals and fractions. It is important that students understand percentages, not only to demonstrate proficiency in this particular grade level, but also in subsequent grades and in the student's future. In addition, students will encounter percentages in other academic areas, such as literacy (comparisons, data) and social sciences (economic trends and transactions, statistics). So, from this one example of percentages, you can see how it meets all three criteria: **leverage** (knowledge used in multiple academic disciplines), **endurance** (relevant throughout the student's lifetime), and **essentiality** (knowledge necessary for student to succeed in the next grade level).*

A common stumbling block for teachers is that, all too often, teachers will want to include many, if not all of the outcomes as key concepts. However, this is not the intent of what a key concept is or how it assists us in supporting our students. We have to be diligent in examining the curriculum to identify those outcomes that have the greatest impact. We can identify these key concepts through assessment data (classroom, school, and/or district level), observational trends over the years (if experienced with the grade level), and collaboration with other teachers (same grade or across grade levels). Typically, we want to identify six to eight key concepts for each grade level.

It is important to note two points related to key concepts. First, key concepts are outcomes that have a high level of importance and come directly from the curriculum. They are not add-ons but are instead designed to provide a way to approach instruction and learning that will optimize student engagement. Second, a focus on key concepts does not, and should not, preclude working with all other required curriculum outcomes. It is necessary that we address all outcomes in the classroom so that we are not creating any gaps in student learning.

As this book is structured by grade ranges, the sections with more than one grade level (Grades 1 to 3 and Grades 4 to 6) will have more than six to eight key concepts, as these concepts will be representative of multiple grades.

List of Key Concepts by Grade Range

As previously stated, there will be three grade ranges for this book: Kindergarten, Primary (Grades 1 to 3), and Elementary (Grades 4 to 6). I have grouped key concepts within central ideas for the purpose of highlighting the interconnectedness of mathematical concepts. And, as a way to assist teachers in working with their own provincial curriculum, I have used the curricular strands as a way to organize the content within the grade ranges.

Before sharing the key concepts for each of the grade ranges described in the introduction, I want to make note of terminology. Depending on your jurisdiction, curriculum strands are referred to differently. For this reason, please take note of the following:

- **Number** is commonly used throughout the country.
- **Algebra** is interchangeable with **Patterning** and with **Patterns & Relations**.
- **Spatial Sense** is interchangeable with **Shape & Space** and with **Geometry & Measurement**.
- **Data** is interchangeable with **Statistics & Probability**.
- **Financial Literacy** is a stand-alone strand within a few provinces but is only referenced within other strands by the remaining provinces.

Kindergarten Key Concepts	
Number	• Subitize • Number Sequence • Count a Collection • Represent a Number • Partition Numbers • Compare Numbers

Algebra (Patterns & Relations)	**Patterns** • Identify and Describe Repeating Patterns
Spatial Sense (Shape & Space)	**Measurement** • Compare Objects Using Measurement

Primary (Grades 1-3) Key Concepts	

Number	**Count**
	• Number Sequence
	• Count a Collection
	
	Estimate Quantities
	• Estimate Using Referents
	
	Whole Numbers
	• Represent Numbers
	• Partition Numbers
	• Compare Numbers
	• Place Value
	
	Fractions
	• Represent Fractions
	• Compare Fractions
	
	Addition & Subtraction
	• Add and Subtract Whole Numbers
	  • Solve
	  • Estimate
	• Mental Math: Fact Learning
	
	Multiplication & Division
	• Multiply and Divide Whole Numbers
	  • Solve

Algebra (Patterns & Relations)	**Patterns** • Identify and Describe Patterns **Solve Equations** • Solve Equations with Symbols
Spatial Sense (Shape & Space)	**Measurement** • Find the Length • Find the Perimeter

Data	Data Management
(Statistics & Probability)	• Collect, Record, Organize, and Analyze Data
Financial Literacy	**Money Concepts** • Identify Different Ways to Represent Amounts of Money

	Elementary (Grades 4-6) Key Concepts

Number	**Whole Numbers**
	• Represent Numbers
	• Partition Numbers
	• Compare Numbers
	• Place Value
	
	Decimals
	• Represent Numbers
	• Partition Numbers
	• Compare Numbers
	• Place Value
	
	Fractions
	• Represent Fractions
	• Compare Fractions
	
	Relate Numbers
	• Relate Fractions, Decimal Numbers, and Percent
	
	Integers
	• Represent Integers
	• Compare Integers
	
	Addition & Subtraction
	• Add and Subtract Whole Numbers
	  • Solve
	  • Estimate
	• Add and Subtract Decimal Numbers
	  • Solve
	  • Estimate
	
	Multiplication & Division
	• Multiply and Divide Whole Numbers
	  • Solve
	  • Estimate
	• Multiply and Divide Decimal Numbers
	  • Solve

	• Estimate • Mental Math: Fact Learning
Algebra (Patterns & Relations)	**Solve Equations** • Solve Equations with Variables
Spatial Sense (Shape & Space)	**Measurement** • Find the Perimeter, Area, and Volume **Geometry** • Measure Angles
Data (Statistics & Probability)	**Data Management** • Collect, Record, Organize, and Analyze Data Using Graphs
Financial Literacy	**Cost of Transactions** • Estimate and Calculate Cost of Transactions

2

Problem Types

Take a moment and think of a problem that you would assign to your students. It can be addressing any concept(s) you wish.

Now, I want you to stop and consider the following questions:

- Did you craft that problem yourself or did you select it from a resource?
- Why did you select that problem?
- What is your intended learning goal with that particular problem?
- What will success look like in terms of solving that problem?
- What conversations would you hope stem from working on this problem?
- How would you facilitate these conversations?

After considering your problem and the responses to the questions above, how do you feel? I wanted to start this chapter with this scenario because the problems we assign in our classes influence the learning experiences students have and their perceptions of math and themselves as mathematicians.

Too often we pull problems from resources and use them solely to address the concept that is the lesson focus. But we may be giving ourselves more work in the long-term than if we had taken a bit more time to consider the problem, what purpose it is serving, and how it will extend student learning.

Let's go back to the problem you thought of at the beginning of this chapter. Does it have the following three characteristics (Greenwald, 2000)?

- **Initial state:** What is presented to the student at the onset of the problem-solving experience.
- **Goal state:** The preferred outcome of the problem.
- **Obstacles:** The stumbling blocks that occur between the initial state and goal state.

If it does, your problem would be categorized as a defined problem, but if it is missing one or more of these characteristics, it would be categorized as an ill-defined problem (Costello, 2022).

While you may not be familiar with the terminology of defined and ill-defined problems, it is important to recognize the difference between the two and ensure that students engage with both categories of problems. Recall my analogy of fiction and non-fiction in the introduction: while there are similarities, there are also contrasts in text structure, how information is presented, and what is expected from the reader when engaging with the text. Thus, if one type of text was omitted from a student's reading experience, they would be missing out on the aspects specific to that textual type. It would be the same in terms of problems: if students are only working with one category of problems (defined or ill-defined), they are missing out on problem-solving opportunities. Let's take a look at these two categories of problems.

Defined Problems

Problems that have these three characteristics are categorized as defined problems: an initial state, goal state, and obstacles. By having these characteristics, a problem contains all the information a student would need to solve it (Costello, 2022; English, Fox & Watters, 2005). It is also important to note that some defined problems will have a contextual element while others will not.

There are multiple types of defined problems, as can be seen in the visual below (Costello, 2022):

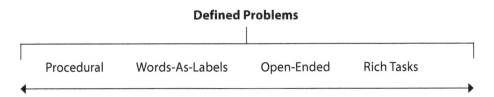

Procedural

Procedural problems do not contain a context. Students are provided with a prompt, typically where the strategy is already identified, and they must apply the steps accurately in order to find the solution (Costello, 2022).

There can be variety in the procedural problems assigned to students. For now, however, I want to share a single example of a procedural problem for each grade range:

Kindergarten	Primary (Grades 1–3)	Elementary (Grades 4–6)
	9 = ? + 5	14.9 + 3.08

Words-as-Labels

Words-as-labels problems, commonly referred to as **word problems** or **story problems**, provide context for students. Students must read through the problem and decide which strategy applies to the situation. They must then apply this strategy to solve the problem.

There can be variety in the words-as-labels problems assigned to students, both in terms of content and structure. For example, they can contain extraneous information, charts and tables that display important information, pictures meant to aid in supplying a context and/or providing information, and multiple steps. For now, however, I want to share a single example of a words-as-labels problem for each grade range:

Kindergarten	Primary (Grades 1–3)	Elementary (Grades 4–6)
Students found three frisbees to play with during recess. If there needs to be five frisbees for the game, how many more frisbees do the students need?	A rectangular bulletin board was put up outside of the local art studio. What is the perimeter of this bulletin board if the width is 125 cm and the length is 400 cm?	A hockey player needed to buy a new stick and helmet for the upcoming season. The price of the stick is $108.95 and the price of the helmet is $215.95. All prices include taxes. If the player had $340.00, how much money would they have after the purchase?

Open-ended Problems

Open-ended problems and rich tasks are often thought of synonymously. For the purpose of this book, I distinguish the two based on context. Open-ended problems do not provide context whereas rich tasks do.

Open-ended problems, commonly referred to as **open questions**, provide students with a greater degree of choice in both strategy selection and application. They are constructed in a way that allows for multiple possible solving methods and answers (Small, 2013).

There can be various degrees of openness within open-ended problems. For now, however, I want to share a single example of an open-ended problem for each grade range:

Kindergarten	Primary (Grades 1–3)	Elementary (Grades 4–6)
I have three colors that make a repeating pattern. What could my pattern look like?	I have an increasing pattern. The fourth number in the pattern is 36. What could the first three numbers be?	The product of two whole numbers is a three-digit number. What are the two numbers and the product?

Rich Tasks

Rich tasks are problems that are accessible to all learners. They provide the opportunity for students to select from a variety of approaches and representations to work through the problem, and one or more solutions can exist (National Council of Teachers of Mathematics, 2014; Van de Walle, Karp, Bay-Williams & McGarvey, 2017). A key aspect of rich tasks is the opportunity for extension so that students can continue exploration if they choose to (Costello, 2022). Typically, rich tasks are framed within familiar contexts so that students can relate them to experiences or situations they have had inside or outside of school.

There can be variety in the rich tasks assigned to students, both in terms of content and structure. Here is an example of a rich task for each grade range:

Kindergarten	Primary (Grades 1–3)	Elementary (Grades 4–6)
There are two towers of blocks on a table. One tower is red while the other tower is green. The green tower is much taller than the red tower. How many blocks could be in each tower?	On my way to school, I noticed that I had a collection of coins in my pocket. There were nickels, dimes, and quarters. I had between 90 cents and one dollar. What coins could I have had?	A group of students are creating a mural for the entry way of the school. The only three parameters put in place by the teacher are 1) the mural must reflect school spirit, 2) the mural must be rectangular in shape, and 3) the area must be between 120 and 200 square centimeters. What could the dimensions of the mural be?

Ill-Defined Problems

English Language Learners (ELL) tend to struggle with the textual demands presented within problems. It is not uncommon to observe that ELL have more proficiency with procedural than they do with the other defined problems. The context given in words-as-labels problems and rich tasks may be unfamiliar to ELL and can often create a stumbling block to engagement.

In terms of ill-defined problems, there does not have to be a lot of text. If carefully crafted to reflect a meaningful context for ELL, ill-defined problems can be a great tool to leverage mathematical understanding without getting lost in textual demands and unfamiliar context.

It is typical to hear teachers communicating their lack of familiarity and comfort with ill-defined problems. This stems from their lack of experience with such problems, both from their time as a student and their time as a teacher. Regardless of this unfamiliarity and discomfort, we have to appreciate that ill-defined problems are in a category of their own and that these problems play an important part in student learning. Consider the visual below (Costello, 2022).

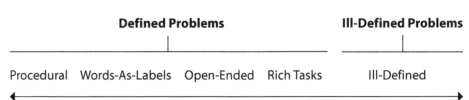

Ill-defined problems are missing one or more of the three characteristics of a problem (initial state, goal state, obstacles). The purpose for omitting one of more of these characteristics is to have problems resembling the real world (Costello, 2022). Because they are missing one or more of these characteristics, ill-defined problems are typically thought to be messier than defined problems.

Students must take on an independent role when working with ill-defined problems. The initial state tends to be quite vague and limited, and the information necessary to solve the problem is not as forthcoming as it is in defined problems. Along with this, ill-defined problems rarely provide a specific goal state. Due to this ambiguity and vagueness, the student must play an active role in structuring the problem. As such, the goal state is influenced and therefore determined by the student. Because the student plays such an active role in the process, their level of engagement, **autonomy**, and problem-solving ability is heightened as they enter, work through, and solve the problem.

Ill-defined problems can take on many forms and can look quite different from one to the other. However, one commonality with all ill-defined problems is that there is a contextual element. This contextual element provides students with various points of entry to approach, work through, and solve the problem. Here is a single example of an ill-defined problem for each grade range:

Kindergarten	Primary (Grades 1–3)	Elementary (Grades 4–6)
Our class just completed an art project and we are eager to share our work. It would be great to have an open house, but we must organize it and decide how many people would be at such an event.	Mathematicians use a lot of different tools when solving problems. Knowing that we have limited space in our math center, we need to decide on which tools would be most used by students.	Our community is looking into after-school programs but wants to make sure that they are appropriate for our youth. They are looking for help.

Before we leave this introduction of ill-defined problems, I want to highlight a feature of this problem type that is unlike any of the other problems I have shared. You will have noticed that there is no question explicitly stated at the end of the problem. There is a significant level of ambiguity and vagueness within an ill-defined problem. As such, the student must bring a lot of their own experiences to both shaping and solving the problem. Because of this, the focus with ill-defined problems tends to be on which concept or concepts students select to solve the problem. It is the student(s) deciding which concept(s) to apply rather than the teacher deciding which concept(s) the student will practice.

Toolbox of Problems

There is no magic number as to how many of each problem type students should be assigned. Generally, students will have many opportunities to engage with defined problems. What is important, however, is that students are provided some opportunities with ill-defined problems as well.

The intent of this chapter was to provide an overview of the two categories of problems (defined and ill-defined), and how there must be a variety of problems offered to students. When offered such a variety of problems, the teacher can account for numerous problem-solving scenarios and can address the learning needs of all students.

The remainder of this book provides multiple examples of the problems highlighted within this chapter for each of the key concepts. Accompanying this bank of problems are suggestions for placement within lessons, as well as teacher moves so that the reader can easily identify a plan to use these problems in their classroom.

Please Take Note

Some of the key concepts that we will explore within this book do not align very well with some of the problem types. In such cases, the key concept may align only a little bit or not at all. For key concepts that align only a little bit with a problem type, there may be limited examples of the specific problem type (e.g., one to two examples). For key concepts that do not align with a problem type, I make an explicit note.

As noted in the overview of ill-defined problems, an ill-defined problem is not so much the student(s) practicing a key concept predetermined by the teacher as it is the student(s) deciding which concept(s) applies to their framing of the ill-defined problem. Therefore, there is great variability in what key concept students may apply to the ill-defined problem. I make note of these occurrences when addressing those key concepts and problem types.

You will notice that some ill-defined problems apply to multiple key concepts. In such instances, I make a note. Some teachers may choose not to use the same question for multiple key concepts, while others may choose to revisit the question and use it as an opportunity to approach a solution using a different concept. This will provide students the opportunity to make connections and observe how problems can be approached from a range of concepts. Revisiting ill-defined problems also can foster confidence and risk-taking in students as they have prior knowledge and experience with this question to draw upon.

This can be seen as another aspect of the messiness of math.

3

Kindergarten

This chapter is dedicated to the key concepts learned in Kindergarten. As stated in Chapter 1, the concepts are categorized by strand. Based on your jurisdiction, the magnitude of the number explored within the key concept may differ (i.e., instead of numbers up to 10, it may be numbers up to 20). Regardless of the curriculum you follow, be mindful that the numbers 5 and 10 are important benchmarks. You should be encouraging students to explore and strengthen their capacity with these two benchmarks before moving on to numbers above 10.

For each key concept, I provide a brief overview, *look fors*, and common misconceptions. In addition to this important information, I also provide a suggestion as to where in the lesson such problems may fit (i.e., warm-up, independent practice, consolidation).

Kindergarten Key Concepts	
Number	• Subitize • Number Sequence • Count a Collection • Represent a Number • Partition Numbers • Compare Numbers
Algebra (Patterns & Relations)	**Patterns** • Identify and Describe Repeating Patterns
Spatial Sense (Shape & Space)	**Measurement** • Compare Objects Using Measurement

This chapter is also meant to be practical so that educators can strengthen their understanding of the key concepts and have a large number of problems that they can bring into the classroom. These problems will be reflective of the different problem types explained in Chapter 2. Please note, however, that not all key concepts align with all problem types. Omissions are highlighted throughout this chapter.

When considering problem types for Kindergarten, please take note:

- **Procedural problems** can be used throughout a math lesson. In Kindergarten, teachers typically use them during teacher-led individual or small-group sessions, math interviews, and independent practice.
- **Words-as-labels problems** can be used for warm-up, math centers, and individual or small-group sessions. More and more, teachers are relying on this problem type to consolidate learning.
- **Open-ended problems** can be used throughout a lesson and are great for **differentiation**. They can also be used to launch a lesson, provide structure for math centers, and generate discourse during consolidation.
- **Rich tasks** are typically used within the independent part of a lesson. This problem type provides a great opportunity for students to engage with a concept for a duration of time. Much of the work done within rich tasks form the basis of the **consolidation block**.
- **Ill-defined problems** form the basis of the independent part of a lesson. Similar to rich tasks, this problem type provides a great opportunity for students to engage with a concept for an extended period of time. The thinking done with ill-defined problems forms the basis of the consolidation block.

After each key concept you'll find suggested teacher moves to aid students in developing their problem-solving abilities and next steps.

Number: Subitize

Be sure to refer to your curriculum for grade-specific expectations

Brief Overview	Look Fors	Common Misconceptions
• Subitizing is the ability to tell how many there are without having to count. It is seeing "at a glance."	• Students briefly look (3 seconds or less) at an arrangement of items or dots, and identify the number represented without counting.	• Students are unable to see at a glance. • Students only count to determine total.

Problem Types

Procedural Problems

- Use your fingers to represent a quantity. Ask students, without counting, to tell you how many fingers you are holding up.
- Display a number represented on a five frame. Ask students to say how many there are on the five frame without having to count.
- Display a number represented on a ten frame. Ask students to say how many there are on the ten frame without having to count.

- Have students roll a number cube with dot arrangements. Ask students to say the number rolled without counting the dots.
- Display a dot card to students. Ask students to make the dot pattern they saw using counters.

Words-as-Labels Problems

- While playing a game, you roll a numbered cube. Without counting, how many dots do you see when it stops rolling?

- We have to make a picture that represents 6. But, it has to be made so that people won't have to count what's in the picture to know it represents 6.

Open-Ended Problems

- Ask students to select a number and arrange counters in a way that will make it easy to recognize. Get them to explain their thinking.
- Ask students to select a number and arrange counters in a way that will make it difficult to recognize. Get them to explain their thinking.
- Using colored counters, ask students to show you three different arrangements that represent a particular number.
- Show a set of dot plates that all show the same number except for one card. Ask students to tell you which dot card does not belong in the set.
- Ask students to name two numbers that are easy to recognize on a ten frame.

Rich Tasks

- Three students were discussing the number 5. Each of the students said that they could show 5 in a way that would make it easy for people to see. Are they correct? Are there more ways to show 5?
- Some students at school are having trouble recognizing certain numbers. Can you create a picture that would help them understand? It will be used in the hallway during group work. What should the picture look like? Explain why.
- The world we live in can help us make sense of math. Think about things in our school and community that when we see we can easily recognize the quantity of without having to count. Use these items and images to make a book of numbers.
- Sam and Cody want to make dot plates with the numbers 1 to 10. They think that using two different colors of stickers on each dot plate will help their classmates see the numbers more clearly. Show how they can make the dot plates.

Ill-Defined Problems

Ill-defined problems are not typically applied to this particular key concept. However, students may engage in subitizing as they work through ill-defined problems for other key concepts.

Teacher Moves

Questions:

- How did you see that number?
- Did you see smaller parts within the whole?
- Were there certain arrangements that made the number easier to see?
- Have you seen that arrangement outside of school?

Next Steps:

- If students are struggling with subitizing, focus on arrangements that may be more familiar to them (dot arrangement on dice, five frames, and ten frames). Encourage other students and yourself, as well, to share how you saw the number without having to count.
- Once students make progress, do an inventory of the numbers they can identify. If some numbers are showing some progress, focus on those first.

Number: Number Sequence

Be sure to refer to your curriculum for grade-specific expectations

Brief Overview	Look Fors	Common Misconceptions
• **Rote counting** is the ability to recite the number sequence. • Rote counting includes the number sequence both forward and backward. • Rote counting to a specified number should be mastered prior to counting quantities to that specified number.	• Students correctly say the number sequence, forward and backward, without the use of a number line, hundreds chart, etc. • Students correctly write the number sequence, forward and backward, without the use of a number line, hundreds chart, etc. • Students correctly identify errors in a number sequence without the use of a number line, hundreds chart, etc.	• Students inaccurately recall number sequence. • Students have difficulty saying the number sequence backward.

Problem Types

Procedural Problems

- Start at 0 and count forward to 10.
- Start at 10 and count backward to 0.
- Start at 3 and count forward to 10.
- Start at 7 and count backward to 0.
- Start at 4 and count forward to 7.
- Start at 9 and count backward to 3.
- Identify and correct the error in the following number sequence:
    9, 8, 6, 5, 4, 3, 2, 1

Words-as-Labels Problems

- In class, a student was asked to count forward from the number 7. What will be the next number the student says?
- In class, a student was asked to count backward from the number 6. What will be the next number the student says?
- When counting backward, Julio had to pause and think about what came after 4. Finish the number sequence to 1.
- When counting forward, Emma had to pause and think about what came after 5. Finish the number sequence to 10.
- The teacher asked a student if he would say the number 7 if asked to count backward from 6. Would the student say 7 in this number sequence? Explain your thinking.
- The teacher asked a student if she would say the number 4 if asked to count forward from 3. Would the student say 3 in this number sequence? Explain your thinking.

Open-Ended Problems

- Choose a number to start counting forward from. What is the next number you will say?
- Choose a number to start counting backward from. What is the next number you will say?
- Choose a number to start counting forward from. Name a number that you will say later in the counting sequence.
- Choose a number to start counting backward from. Name a number that you will say later in the counting sequence.
- Name a number. Share a counting sequence that will have that number said right away.

Rich Tasks

- You and another classmate take turns counting. Sometimes, when you start at the same number, you both say the same numbers when continuing to count. Other times, when you say the same number, you both say different numbers when continuing to count. How is this possible? Explain your thinking.
- Consider a number that is meaningful to you. Find a partner and share your number and why it is meaningful. How are the two numbers similar? How are the two numbers different?

Ill-Defined Problems

Ill-defined problems are not typically applied to this particular key concept. However, students can recite the number sequence as they work with ill-defined problems for other key concepts.

Teacher Moves

Questions:

- Do you find certain parts of the number sequence more difficult to remember?
- What strategies do you use when you have to start counting at a number other than 1?
- Do you prefer counting forward or backward?

Next Steps:

- If students are struggling with the number sequence, get a baseline as to what numbers they can count. Then, continually add greater numbers as they master new ones.
- If students are mixing up counting forward and counting backward, focus on one number sequence and solidify that for students.
- When working on both counting forward and counting backward, work with numbers 1 to 5. When those are mastered, then move onto numbers 1 to 10.

Number: Count a Collection

Be sure to refer to your curriculum for grade-specific expectations

Brief Overview	Look Fors	Common Misconceptions

• Students can say/record the number that represents the quantity in a given collection.	• Students can apply the counting principles:
	  • One number is said for each item in the group and is counted once.
	  • Counting begins with the number 1 and follows the traditional number sequence.
	  • The quantity in the set is the last number said.
	  • The starting point and order of counting the objects does not affect the quantity.
	  • The arrangement or types of objects does not affect the count.
	  • It does not matter what is being counted, the count will always be the same.
		• Students are missing one of the counting principles.

Problem Types

Procedural Problems

- Provide students with a set of 7 items. Ask students to count the items and tell you how many are in the set.

- Provide students with a set of 9 items. Ask students to count the items. Ask students to show you 9. Note whether students point to the last item counted or whether they show the set of 9 items.
- Ask students to count a set of items. Once they finish counting, ask them how many are in the set. Move the items around and ask them if there is still the same amount. Note whether students automatically recall the same amount or whether they have to count the set again.
- Ask students to take a handful of linking cubes. Ask students to count the linking cubes and say how many cubes they have.
- Provide students with a row of two-sided counters. The first six counters are yellow and the last three are red. Ask students to count the counters starting at red. Note whether students stop counting at the third red counter or if they wrap around to the yellow to count the whole set.

Words-as-Labels Problems

- The following coats were left on the floor:

  How many coat hooks are needed so that the coats on the floor can have a place to be hung?
- While on the school bus, a student noticed the following:

  How many birds did the student see?
- A student wanted to build towers with blocks. How many blocks did the student use when building towers?

Open-Ended Problems

- Direct students to grab a handful of linking cubes. Ask students how many linking cubes they picked up.
- Ask students if the total in a collection would be different if they started counting at different items. Explain their thinking.

Rich Tasks

- Two students were asked to count all the marbles in a collection. After counting the collection, Susie said there were 6 marbles. After Paul counted the collection, he said there were 7 marbles. Can they both be correct? Explain your thinking.

- Students were given different collections to count. Thom's collection was in a small box. Jaya's collection was stored in a large bag. Thom said his collection had less than Jaya's. Jaya disagreed. Without counting either collection, explain why both students could be correct in their thinking.
- You are working with the numbers 1 to 10. To demonstrate your understanding of counting, you want to make a number book that contains the appropriate amount of items for each number. Make this book and share your thinking.

Ill-Defined Problems

- We need to replace some of the supplies in the Free Play Center. Let's figure it out together.

Teacher Moves

Questions:

- How do you keep track of the items you count?
- What would happen to the count if I moved items?
- Would there still be _____ if I started counting this item first?

Next Steps:

- It is crucial that students can recite the number sequence prior to counting items. Start with the number sequence if not mastered.
- Identify the counting principles students have mastered.
- If students are struggling to accurately count a collection up to 10, focus on collections of 1 to 5.
- If students are struggling with counting pictures, revert back to concrete items that they can physically manipulate as they count.

Number: Represent a Number

Be sure to refer to your curriculum for grade-specific expectations

Brief Overview	Look Fors	Common Misconceptions
• Numbers can be represented in five ways: contextually, concretely, pictorially, symbolically, and verbally.	• Students can accurately represent a given number using pictures and concrete objects. • Examples are five frames, ten frames, manipulatives, fingers, drawings. • Students can find an example of a given number in the environment.	• Students are not matching quantity to the given number.

Problem Types

Procedural Problems

- Show the number 8 with fingers.
- Show the number 4 using any item.
- Represent the number 7 on a ten frame.
- Draw a picture that represents 9 balloons.
- Represent the number 6 using a numeral.
- Identify the number 6 within our classroom.
- Identify the number 4 within our school.
- Where do you see numbers around our community?

Words-as-Labels Problems

- A local artist wants a picture of six trees. How could she draw it?
- The school team scored 7 goals during their last game. Using a ten frame, represent the number seven.
- It was time for centers. The teacher called Sabrina, Alex, Talia, and Xavier to the art table. Using your fingers, show the number of students called to the art table.
- There are three empty coat hooks outside of the classroom. Draw a picture of a coat for each empty hook.
- A group of children took part in a building contest. As part of the contest, students needed to build towers using nine blocks. Create a collection of nine blocks for the group of children.

Open-Ended Problems

- It takes two hands to represent a number. What could the number be?
- There are more empty spaces than filled spaces on a ten frame. What is the number?
- Say a number that you see in the classroom. Explain what it means.
- Represent a number of your choice. Why did you pick this number?
- A number can be represented on a ten frame. What is the number?

Rich Tasks

- Ten frames can also be used to represent two numbers. How is this possible? Show your thinking.
- The world we live in can help us make sense of math. Think about things in our school and community that represent numbers. Use these items and images to make a book of numbers.
- Consider a number between 1 and 10 that is meaningful to you. Show this number in four ways. What are the similarities in the four ways that you represented the number? What are the differences in the four ways that you represented the number?

Ill-Defined Problems

- The librarian is only in the library for some of the day and he wants help in making a system that shares the number of books written by authors. The purpose of this system is to assist students in seeing that popular authors typically have written more than one book.

Teacher Moves

Questions:

- What number have you represented?
- Why did you choose to represent that number the way you did?

Next Steps:

- If students are not matching the correct quantity to the given number, ensure that they can correctly identify the number.
- If students are having difficulty matching the correct quantity to the given number, ensure that they can accurately apply the counting principles.
- If students are struggling with representing numbers, identify the numbers they can represent and then build from that (start with numbers 1 to 5 and then build toward 1 to 10).

Number: Partition Numbers

Be sure to refer to your curriculum for grade-specific expectations

Brief Overview	Look Fors	Common Misconceptions
• The ability to recognize that any number can be partitioned into two smaller numbers.	• Students can show a given number (whole) as two parts and name the number of items in each part. • Students can identify a number (whole) that is represented in two parts. • Students recognize that partitioning a number (whole) into two parts does not affect the count.	• The two parts do not add to equal the whole. • Students do not trust that whole remains the same once broken into parts.

Problem Types

Procedural Problems

- Find the missing part:

8	
6	?

- Show the number 7 in two parts.
- Find the missing whole:

?	
3	3

- Does the total count remain the same if we break 4 into 1 and 3? Explain.
- The following visual represents the whole. What could two parts be?

Words-as-Labels Problems

- Students found three frisbees to play with during recess. If there needs to be five frisbees for the game, how many more frisbees do the students need?
- There are eight linking cubes on the floor. Four of the linking cubes are yellow. The other linking cubes on the floor are blue. How many blue linking cubes are on the floor?
- While playing dominoes, a player realized that the two numbers showing on his first domino were 5 and 3. How many dots were on the domino?
- The library received book donations. Four books were donated by the principal and three books were donated by the bus driver. How many books were donated to the library?
- There are seven birthday cards on the shelf. Three of the cards are from family while the others are from friends. How many cards are from friends?

Open-Ended Problems

- Select a domino. Identify the whole for the two given parts.
- Two parts are the same number. What could the whole be?
- The two parts are different numbers. What could the whole be?
- A whole is broken into two parts. One part is really close to the whole. What could the two parts and whole be?
- One of part of a whole is 3. What could the other part and the whole be?

Rich Tasks

- You have counters on your desk. Some counters fall onto the floor. Now, there are some counters on the desk and some counters on the floor. How many are on the floor and how many are on your desk? How many counters do you have altogether?
- You and a partner each have a collection of linking cubes. When you each break apart your collection, sometimes you have the same amounts in each part and other times the amounts in each part are different. Do you each have the same number of linking cubes in your collection? Explain your thinking.
- You notice that there are many ways to break a number into two parts. What could the whole number be? Explain your thinking.
- When you break a number into two smaller parts, you notice that the two parts are close together in the number sequence. What could the whole number and two smaller parts be?

Ill-Defined Problems

- We need new supplies for two of our centers. As a class, we can only order a handful of items at a time. What items will we order and how will we make sure that both centers receive some of the items?

Teacher Moves

Questions:

- What number have you partitioned?
- What are the two parts?
- How many do you have if you combine the two parts? (Do students need to count or do they automatically know it is the whole number?)
- Are there more than two ways to break apart the whole?

Next Steps:

- If students cannot break apart numbers, start with small numbers.
- If students are struggling to know that the two parts combined is the whole number, use one set of concrete objects for the whole. Then, as you partition the whole into two parts, emphasize that you are still using the same number of objects just rearranging them into smaller numbers.
- I find that if students struggle with partitioning numbers, use students as examples for part-part-whole. Then, move to manipulatives. Sometimes the move to pictures is too quick and this can hinder student understanding.

Number: Compare Numbers

Be sure to refer to your curriculum for grade-specific expectations

Brief Overview	Look Fors	Common Misconceptions

• The comparison of numbers is based on quantity (concrete objects or pictorial representations).
 • There is a progression in mathematical language.
   • Initially, terms such as **more, less, same, enough,** and **not enough** are acceptable.
   • Eventually, move towards **equal, greater than,** and **less than** when comparing numbers.
	• Students can use one of two strategies to compare the quantities within two collections:
	   • Use structure to align the collections and compare (**one-to-one correspondence**).
	   • Count to identify which collection has a greater number (eventually, students can use benchmarks of 5, 10, etc.) (**positions in counting sequence**).
		• Students are unable to compare two collections (difficulty in lining up the collections one-to-one or having difficulty with counting sequence).

Problem Types

Procedural Problems

- Which number is greater: 7 or 3? Show your thinking.
- What number is less: 2 or 4? Show your thinking.
- How can you explain that 5 is more than 4?
- Make a set of dots that is the same as this set:

- Make a set of dots with more than this set:
  ♦♦♦♦♦♦

Words-as-Labels Problems

- There are 4 red blocks and 3 yellow blocks on the table. Are there more red or yellow blocks on the table?
- Tomas drew 8 pictures. Ali drew 6 pictures. Did Tomas or Ali draw more pictures?
- There are 5 stools and 4 chairs in the reading center. Are there more stools or chairs?
- There are 6 chocolate chip cookies and 6 sugar cookies. Are there more chocolate chip cookies or sugar cookies?
- A teacher read 4 books to her class and the school librarian read 7 books. Who read fewer books?

Open-Ended Problems

- I have two numbers. One is bigger than the other. What are my two numbers?
- When I count, I say one number near the beginning and one near the end. What are my two numbers?
- How are 4 and 6 different?
- Place 5 counters on the plate. Ask students to make a set that has less counters than the 5 counters on the plate.
- Roll a number cube. Make a number less than the rolled number.

Rich Tasks

- There are two towers of blocks on a table. One tower is red while the other tower is green. The green tower is much taller than the red tower. How many blocks could be in each tower?
- You have two numbers to compare. One of the numbers is much closer to 10 than the other. What are your two numbers and which one is bigger?
- You choose two numbers. You want to show your friends that the two numbers are close to each other. How can you arrange items to show your friends this comparison?
- You choose two numbers. You want to show your friends that the two numbers are not close to each other. How can you arrange items to show your friends this comparison?

Ill-Defined Problems

- There are several books in our classroom that need to be removed from the reading center. However, we only want to remove the books that are the lesser preferred books. Can we identify the books that need to stay and the books that need to be removed?

Teacher Moves

Questions:

- Which number is bigger? How did you decide that was the bigger number?
- Which number is smaller? How did you decide that was the smaller number?

Next Steps:

- Sometimes when students struggle with comparing numbers, it is that they are struggling with the number sequence. Ensure they can properly recite numbers if they are using this comparison method.
- If students struggle with comparing numbers, use a one-to-one comparison of items. Ensure students are aligning the two items properly. Also, ensure that the items being used to compare are the same size, otherwise students will pick the number represented by the larger sized item.

Algebra: Identify and Describe Repeating Patterns

Be sure to refer to your curriculum for grade-specific expectations

Brief Overview	Look Fors	Common Misconceptions
• Within a repeating pattern (of only two to three elements), there is repetition. The shortest string of elements that repeat is referred to as the **core**. • Patterns can be auditory or visual; and, such patterns can be represented with material, sound, and/or movement. • It may be helpful to introduce a **letter code** when describing the pattern (i.e., ABABAB).	• For a given repeating pattern, students can: • Identify the core. • Extend the repeating pattern. • Reproduce the repeating pattern in another representation (visual, sound, movement, etc.). • Students can create a repeating pattern (of two to three elements).	• Students cannot identify the core of the pattern. • Students cannot extend the pattern. • Students cannot reproduce the pattern in another representation.

Problem Types

Procedural Problems

- What comes next in the following pattern?
  ✓✓✗✓✓✗✓✓✗✓✓✗✓✓✗
- What is the core in the following pattern?

- Recreate the following pattern using sounds.
  ✓✓✗✗✓✓✗✗✓✓✗✗
- Ask students to describe a pattern that they see in the classroom.
- What is the missing item in the repeating pattern?
  ☼ ⌒ ☼ ⌒ ☼ ⌒ ? ⌒ ☼ ⌒ ☼

Words-as-Labels Problems

- An artist decided to use a patterned border to decorate a bulletin board:

  ★ ♥ ♦ ★ ♥ ♦ ★ ♥ ♦

  What is the core of the pattern in the border?

- In music class, there were three groups of students. The singing group created the following oral pattern:

  Whisper, yell, yell, whisper, yell, yell, whisper, yell, yell

  The dance group said that they reproduced the same pattern using actions:

  Stomp, clap, clap, stomp, clap, clap, stomp, clap, clap

  The teacher asked an art group if they could reproduce the pattern using pictures.

- While waiting in line for music, the first eight students did the following:

  sit, sit, stand, stand, sit, sit, stand, stand

  If the pattern continues, what will the ninth and tenth student be doing?

- A kindergarten class ran out of time when working on a repeating pattern. What picture should be in place of the '?' in the repeating pattern below?

- Some students made a pattern using two shapes, but they are unsure of what comes next. Which shape goes next?

  △○○△○○△○○

Open-Ended Problems

- Three colors are used to make a repeating pattern. What could the pattern look like?
- Make two different patterns using red and blue blocks. What could the two patterns be?
- A repeated pattern is made using three colors of linking cubes. The fourth block in the pattern is the same as the fifth block. What is the pattern?
- The fourth term in a repeating pattern is a square. What is the pattern?
- A pattern has a lot more happy faces than sad faces. What is the pattern?

Rich Tasks

- You found two items to use when making a pattern. You have a lot more of one item than the other. What pattern can you make?
- The teacher shares three items with you: blocks, counters, and crayons. She wants you to make a pattern book showing different patterns. What are the similarities in the patterns you make?
- As part of an art project, your group is assigned to make the border of two bulletin boards. You need to make two different patterns: one for each. What are the similarities and differences in these two patterns?
- You have two items that you want to use to make a pattern. You want the pattern that uses just a few more of one item than another. What does your pattern look like? Explain your thinking in making the pattern.

Ill-Defined Problems

- We need to create a picture that represents our class as learners. The principal wants this picture outside our classroom door. Let's create one that has a pattern in it.

Teacher Moves

Questions:

- What is the repeating pattern?
- What would come next?
- Can we make that pattern using other items?

Next Steps:

- When replicating patterns, leave the original pattern in place and reproduce it directly below. Students can then match items until their comfort level grows.
- If students are having difficulty identifying the core of the pattern, encourage them to chunk the pattern into smaller pieces and to continuously increase the size of the chunk until they find the core.

Spatial Sense: Compare Objects Using Measurement

Be sure to refer to your curriculum for grade-specific expectations

Brief Overview	Look Fors	Common Misconceptions
• Objects are compared by length, mass, and/or volume. • The comparison of the attribute of one object to the same attribute of another object. • Differences are described between objects using words such as **shorter**, **longer**, **taller**, **lighter**, **heavier**, **holds less**, and **holds more**.	• Students will compare the length of two objects visually or by placing them side-by-side. • Students will compare the mass of two objects by using their sense of touch or a balance scale. • Students will compare the volume of two objects by filling up the two objects and seeing which one holds more and which holds less.	• Students do not understand the meaning of the attribute being compared. • Students are not comparing the same attribute. • Students are not aligning the lengths when comparing.

Problem Types

Procedural Problems

- Provide students with pieces of string of different lengths. Ask them which string is shorter.
- Provide students with two bags containing objects of different masses. Ask them which bag is heavier.
- Provide students with two containers. Ask them which container holds more.
- Provide students with two items (e.g., crayon, paper clip, ruler, pencil, glue stick). Ask them to predict and then determine which item is longer.
- Ask students to identify an item that is lighter than themselves. Ask them to explain their thinking.

Words-as-Labels Problems

- There were new pencils and new crayons on the teacher's desk. Students were curious to see which was longer: a new pencil or a new crayon. How can you help them figure it out?
- A group of children received a donation of toys. One child received a basketball while another child received a book. How would you decide which toy was heavier?
- Jayme read in a book that a person's hand was the same length as their foot. Is this true for you? How do you know?
- A basketball and balloon looked to be the same size. How can you figure out which is heavier?
- Two gardeners entered a contest to grow the tallest sunflower. Which gardener had the tallest sunflower and how do you know?

Mr. Smith   Mr. Watts

Open-Ended Problems

- One tower of blocks is a lot taller than another. What could the two towers look like?
- Two containers almost hold the same amount. What could the two containers be?
- One object is a lot heavier than another object. What could the heavier object be?
- Two items are the same length. What could the two items be?
- It is hard to measure the length of two items. What could these two items be?

Rich Tasks

- You need to find two objects in your classroom for a project. One of the objects has to hold a lot more water than the other. What two objects can you select?
- You are building two towers with linking cubes. The two towers are almost the same length. What would you have to do to make them the same length?
- You want to put the counters from the math center into two bags. Your goal is to have one bag a lot heavier than the other bag. Explain your thinking as you work towards your goal.
- The look of objects can be misleading. Find two things in your classroom that look like they have the same mass but are actually very different. What are the two items? Can you explain the difference in mass?

Ill-Defined Problems

- We will be growing plants as part of our science unit. I need help figuring out which type of pot would be best.

Teacher Moves

Questions:

- What two items did you compare? What did you use to compare them?
- What holds more/less, is shorter/longer, or lighter/heavier? How do you know?

Next Steps:

- Encourage students to clearly articulate how they will compare the two items.
- Ensure that:
    - when length is being compared, the objects are aligned properly,
    - when mass is being compared, the scale is accurate, and
    - when volume is being compared, the same measure is being used.

4

Primary (Grades 1–3)

This chapter covers the key concepts used in the Primary level (Grades 1–3). As stated in Chapter 1, the concepts are categorized by strand. For each strand, I have grouped key concepts within central ideas so that teachers can easily sift through this resource to identify problems that address a range of learning needs in the classroom. For example, I've categorized whole numbers as its own group, and list all the relevant key concepts for it. I also have categorized other groups (fractions, addition and subtraction, equations, measurement, etc.), and list all the relevant key concepts for each.

For each key concept, I provide a brief overview, *look fors*, and common misconceptions. In addition, you'll find a suggestion as to where in the lesson such problems may fit (e.g., warm-up, independent practice, or consolidation).

	Primary Key Concepts
Number	**Count** • Number Sequence • Count a Collection **Estimate Quantities** • Estimate Using Referents **Whole Numbers** • Represent Numbers • Partition Numbers • Compare Numbers • Place Value **Fractions** • Represent Fractions • Compare Fractions

Number	**Addition & Subtraction**
	• Add and Subtract Whole Numbers
	  • Solve
	  • Estimate
	• Mental Math: Fact Learning
	
	Multiplication & Division
	• Multiply and Divide Whole Numbers
	  • Solve

Algebra (Patterns & Relations)	**Patterns** • Identify and Describe Patterns **Solve Equations** • Solve Equations with Symbols
Spatial Sense (Shape & Space)	**Measurement** • Find the Length • Find the Perimeter
Data (Statistics & Probability)	**Data Management** • Collect, Record, Organize, and Analyze Data
Financial Literacy	**Money Concepts** • Identify Different Ways to Represent Amounts of Money

This chapter is intended to be practical, so that educators can strengthen their understanding of key concepts and have a large number of problems to bring into the classroom. These problems are not reflective of the different problem types explained in Chapter 2. Please note, however, that not all key concepts align with all problem types. I will highlight any omissions throughout this chapter.

When considering problem types for the primary level (Grades 1–3), please take note:

- **Procedural problems** can be used throughout a math lesson. In the primary level, teachers typically use them during teacher-led individual or small-group sessions, math interviews, and independent practice.
- **Words-as-labels problems** can be used for warm-up, math centers, and individual or small-group sessions. More and more, teachers are relying on this problem type to consolidate learning.
- **Open-ended problems** can be used throughout a lesson and are great for differentiation. They can also be used to launch a lesson, provide structure for math centers, and generate discourse during consolidation.

- **Rich tasks** are typically used within the independent part of a lesson. This problem type provides a great opportunity for students to engage with a concept for a duration of time. Much of the work done within rich tasks form the basis of the consolidation block.
- **Ill-defined problems** form the basis of the independent part of a lesson. Similar to rich tasks, this problem type provides a great opportunity for students to engage with a concept for an extended period of time. The thinking done with ill-defined problems forms the basis of the consolidation block.

After each key concept you'll find suggested teacher moves to aid students in developing their problem-solving abilities and next steps.

Number: Count

Be sure to refer to your curriculum for grade-specific expectations

	Brief Overview	*Look Fors*	**Common Misconceptions**
Number Sequence	• Rote counting is the ability to recite a number sequence. • Rote counting can be counting forward, backwards, and skip counting. Skip counting begins in Grade 1. • Rote counting can entail counting to/ from a specific number. • Rote counting to a specified number should be mastered prior to counting quantities to that specified number.	• Students correctly say the number sequence. • Students correctly write the number sequence. • Students correctly identify errors in a number sequence.	• Students inaccurately recall a number sequence. • Students are unable to count backwards. • Students have difficulty changing decades when recalling the number sequence.
Count a Collection	• Students can say/ record the quantity in a given collection.	• Students can apply the following counting principles: • One number is said for each item in the group and is counted once and only once. • Counting begins with the number 1 and follows the traditional number sequence. • The quantity in the set is the last number said (cardinality). • The starting point and order of counting the objects does not affect the quantity.	• Students cannot accurately apply the counting principles. • Students do not trust the count. • Students have to start back at the number 1 if something is added or taken away from the collection.

		• The arrangement or types of objects does not affect the count. • It does not matter what is being counted, the count will always be the same.	

Problem Types

Procedural Problems

- Start at 0 and count forward to 100.
- Start at 100 and count backward to 0.
- Start at 35 and count forward to 52.
- Start at 73 and count backward to 55.
- Start at 0 and count forward by 2s.
- Start at 76 and count backward by 2s.
- Start at 16 and count forward by 10s.
- Start at 92 and count backward by 10s.
- Identify and correct the error in the following number sequence:
    35, 40, 45, 50, 55, 65, 70, 75, 80
- Count the collection of items.

Words-as-Labels Problems

- An attendee is skip counting the number of people in line for a concert. When counting, the attendee is only saying numbers that end in 0 and 5. What number is the attendee skip counting by?
- A student counted a collection of marbles by 5s. She counted a total of 75. She was recording the numbers as she counted, but her pencil broke at the number 55. What would the last numbers be in the sequence?
- Tai was counting the number of boxes delivered to the skating rink. She decided to count by 2s. She noticed that there were 28 boxes. Record the number sequence that Tai would have said when counting by 2s.
- Alia was having difficulty counting by 2s when she had to start at a number greater than 20. She wanted to practice so that she could do this without needing support.

Open-Ended Problems

- Select two numbers less than 100. Count forward from the smallest number to the largest number.
- Select two numbers less than 100. Count backward from the largest number to the smallest number.
- Select two odd numbers less than 1000. Skip count by 2s forward from the smallest number to the largest number.
- Select two even numbers less than 1000. Skip count by 2s backward from the largest number to the smallest number.
- Select 2, 5, or 10. Start at a number less than 1000 and skip count forward by the number you selected (2, 5, or 10).

- Select 2, 5, or 10. Start at a number less than 1000 and skip count backward by the number you selected (2, 5, or 10).
- You have a collection of items. Count how many is in your collection and record the total.

Rich Tasks

- You and a classmate are asked to count the number of whiteboard markers at the art center. You each notice that there are a lot of markers that need to be counted. You decide to skip count by a larger even number while your classmate skip counts by a smaller even number. Why would each of you make such a decision? What if there are an odd number of markers? Would each of you have the same number of markers that do not fit into a group?
- The librarian asks your reading group to count the number of fiction and non-fiction books that were just returned to the school library. Two of you count the fiction books and another two count the non-fiction books. Counting the fiction books does not take long while counting the non-fiction books takes considerably more time. How many fiction and non-fiction books could there be? What would be the factors that lead to the time difference in counting the books?
- There were some books left on the bookshelf in the school library. When the librarian counted the books one-at-a-time, he discovered there were 93 books. When he counted the same books by 5s, he counted a total of 105. The actual count was 93 books. What could have been the issue when counting by 5s?
- It was time to do an inventory of all baseball equipment in the Phys. Ed department. The teacher asked students to count the number of items that could be used when playing baseball. The students were surprised when they saw how many items there were. Each of the three students decided to count the items in a different way. How many items could have been in the collection and what would the sequence have been for each student's counting?

Ill-Defined Problems

- Soon we will have a party to celebrate all the volunteers that support our class. Each volunteer will get a treat bag as a thank you. Let's start planning what we will put in these treat bags for our volunteers.
- The school librarian was looking for help in determining if there needed to be new books purchased for the school library. In particular, she was wondering about fiction and non-fiction books.

Teacher Moves

Questions:
- Do you find certain parts of the number sequence more difficult to remember?
- What strategies do you use when you have to start counting at a number other than 1?
- Do you prefer counting forward or backward?
- What do you find challenging when skip counting?
- How do you keep track of the items you count?
- What would happen to the count if I moved items?
- Would there still be _____ if I started counting this item first?

Next Steps:

- If students are having difficulty skip counting, ensure that they have the number sequence by 1s.
- If students are having difficult counting backwards, shrink the range of numbers to see what they can do. Then build out from that.
- It is crucial that students can recite the number sequence prior to counting items. Start with the number sequence if not mastered.
- Identify the counting principles students have mastered.
- If students are struggling to accurately count a collection, focus on collections they can count and then extend the size of collection.
- If students are struggling with counting pictures, revert back to concrete items that they can physically manipulate as they count.

Number: Estimate Quantities

Be sure to refer to your curriculum for grade-specific expectations

	Brief Overview	*Look Fors*	**Common Misconceptions**
Estimate Using a Referent	• Estimation with a referent is the ability to identify a quantity with relative accuracy when using a sample group as a reference. • Language associated with estimating includes **more than**, **less than**, **closer to**, and **about**.	• Students can estimate the size of a given collection by comparing it to a **referent**. • Students can select between two possible estimates for a given collection. • Students can rationalize their estimate.	• Students believe that the estimate has to be the same as the actual count. • Students count how many referents instead of recognizing the amount within a referent.

Problem Types

Procedural Problems

- Provide students with a train of 5 linking cubes. Ask students to estimate the number of cubes in a longer train that is on display in the room. Have students explain their thinking.
- Provide students with a collection of 10 paper clips. Inform students that this will be a referent. Now, display a collection of paper clips and ask students to estimate the number of paper clips in this larger collection.
- Show students a group of items and ask them to choose between two given estimates. Have them explain their reasoning for their choice.
- Provide students with a picture of between 100 and 200 counters. Ask students to record an estimate for the number of counters shown. Then, inform students that you are going to show them another picture where 10 of the counters are moved to one side. Ask students if they want to adjust their original estimate and to explain their thinking.

- Provide students with a group of objects (e.g., nickels, crayons, stickers, paper clips, marbles) or pictures showing groups (e.g., people at a game, trucks in a parking lot, books on a table). Ask students how many groups of 10 (or 100) are in the whole group.

Words-as-Labels Problems

- There were boxes of crayons covering the top of Desi's desk. The boxes of crayons were side-by-side, and none were on top of each other. The teacher asked Desi if he thought there would be closer to 100 or 1000 boxes of crayons on the top of the desk. Which estimate do you think would be closer? Explain your thinking.
- A baker was looking at different containers to hold newly baked cookies. He saw a cookie jar as pictured:

- If ten cookies look like this, about how many cookies can be held in the cookie jar?

- The school science club was interested in watching the different kinds of birds flying over the playground. What size of referent would you use if you were asked to estimate the total number of birds flying in the picture below?

- A large number of people were waiting to enter the hockey rink for the provincial championship. The picture below represents the crowd. About how many people will watch the championship game? Explain your thinking.

- A student had drawn dots all over his scribbler page.

- The following is a referent of 10.

- About how many dots are on the page?

Open-Ended Problems

- About how many chapter books could fit in your backpack?
- You have to estimate a quantity consisting of a large number of items. What quantity would you like the referent to represent?
- Your estimate for a quantity is a large 3-digit number. What could you be estimating?
- What could you be estimating if your referent is 5?
- About how many counters can you pick up in ten handfuls?
- Ask students to pick up a handful of linking cubes. Students are to place these linking cubes next to them. Count the number of these cubes as this amount will serve as the referent. Then, provide students with a jug and ask them to fill the jug with linking cubes. Students are to place these linking cubes next to them in a different pile. Ask students to decide how to organize both the referent and the actual jug full of linking cubes so that they can easily use the referent to make an accurate assessment.

Rich Tasks

- A group of students were learning about using referents when estimating. Some of these students argued that referents should only be of 10 while others argued that referents should only be of 100. When would be an appropriate time to use either referent? Are there times when a referent of 10 and a referent of 100 would be helpful?
- You and a friend are asked to estimate the number of attendees at your school's graduation ceremony. If you were to estimate such a large crowd, how large would your referent be and how would you use it to estimate the number of attendees?
- You are asked by your teacher to estimate how many books all of your classmates could fit into their backpacks. How would you determine a referent? What would your estimate be? Explain your thinking.

- You and your class are on a nature walk. You become interested in something you notice and make an estimate. This estimate is a large number. Consider the following questions as it relates to your estimate:
    - What could you have noticed that would make sense for such a large estimate?
    - What size of referent would have made sense?

Ill-Defined Problems

- Our school is raising money for the community youth center. Students and staff want to have a successful yard sale. The principal is looking for help in planning the sale. Specifically, the principal is wondering how many items would be best and how to organize the yard sale.
- Our class is thinking of making cards for random acts of kindness. We want to ensure that we have enough cards, but not too many so that there isn't a lot of waste.

Teacher Moves

Questions:

- How did you arrive at that estimate?
- Did you use a referent when estimating? If yes, what was it and how did you apply it?
- Do you find estimating easier in certain situations vs. others?

Next Steps:

- If students are struggling with estimating, move back to smaller sizes of collections (concrete objects).
- Ensure students can estimate concrete collections before moving to pictorial representations.
- Model and encourage the use of estimation language when estimating.

Number: Whole Numbers

Be sure to refer to your curriculum for grade-specific expectations

	Brief Overview	*Look Fors*	**Common Misconceptions**
Represent Numbers	• Numbers can be represented in five ways: contextually, concretely, pictorially, symbolically, and verbally.	• Students can represent a given number. • Examples are words, expressions, coins, manipulatives, tallies, fingers, or pictures. • Students can translate between and among different representations.	• Students misrepresent the number. • Students are unable to convert between different representations.

Partition Numbers	• The ability to recognize that any number can be partitioned into two or more smaller numbers.	• Students can show a given number (whole) as two or more parts and name each part. • Students can identify a number (whole) that is represented in two or more parts. • Students recognize that partitioning a number (whole) into two or more parts does not affect the count. • Students can represent the given number (whole) as an expression.	• Students do not accurately break the whole into parts. • Students are not confident that the total remains unchanged when broken into parts.

Compare Numbers	• The ability to compare and order numbers.
	• Comparison of numbers is a process that moves from concrete, to pictorial, to symbolic representations.
	• There is a progression in mathematical language.
	  • Initially, terms such as **more, less, same, enough, not enough** are acceptable.
	  • Eventually, move towards **equal, greater than,** and **less than** when comparing numbers.
		• Students can compare numbers concretely (one-to-one), pictorially, using number lines (finding two or more numbers on a number line), with benchmarks, and when comparing digits (left-to-right).
		• Students can order a set of numbers in **ascending** and **descending** order.
		• Students can justify their solutions using benchmarks, hundred charts, number lines, ten-frames, and/or place value.
			• Students use the wrong symbols $(<, >, =)$.
			• Students order numbers the wrong way (ascend/descend).
			• Students inaccurately place numbers on the number line.

Place Value	• **Place value** is a system that explains the value of a digit based on its position in the number.
	• Place value is based on the following principles:
	  • Ten digits (0 to 9).
	  • Each place is ten times the value of the place to the right.
	  • A number has different forms. 135 is 1 hundred, 3 tens, 5 ones and is also 13 tens, 5 ones.
	  • Zero is a place holder.
		• Students can represent a given number using groupable and/or base-ten blocks.
		• Students can identify a number based on a given arrangement of base-ten blocks.
		• Students can represent a given number, in at least two ways, using base-ten blocks.
		• Students can identify the value of a digit in a number.
		• Students can convert a number between standard, expanded, and word form.
			• Students use **face value** with numbers vs. place value (instead of recognizing that the 7 in 78 represents 70, they assume it represents 7).
			• Students have difficulty in converting between word, expanded, and standard form.

Problem Types

Procedural Problems

- Represent 83 in tallies.
- Represent 234 in base-ten blocks.
- Record the value of the underlined digit:
  7<u>6</u>2
- Write the following number in expanded form:
  404
- Order the following numbers in ascending order:
  562, 265, 625, 652, 526
- Partition the following number into two parts:
  153
- Write the following number in standard form and expanded form:
  Three hundred eight

Words-as-Labels Problems

- The librarian opened a box of new books. There were 98 fiction books and 43 non-fiction books. How many books were there altogether?
- A student found four coins in his pocket. There was one nickel, two dimes, and a quarter. How much money did the student have?
- While playing a game, Debra rolled the following three numbers: 5, 3, and 6. What is the largest number Debra could have made with those three numbers?
- Lonnie had found 135 plastic bottles to recycle. His sister, Lucy, found 162 plastic bottles. How many fewer bottles did Lonnie find than Lucy?
- Ty travelled to his grandparent's house in July and his uncle's house in August. The distance to Ty's grandparent's house was 438 km. The distance to Ty's uncle's house was 502 km. How much farther was it for Ty to travel to his uncle's house than his grandparent's house?

Open-Ended Problems

- Use an open number line to place three numbers. Two of the numbers are much larger than the other number.
- Represent a number using 7 base-ten blocks.
- What 2-digit number can you represent using 4 base-ten blocks?
- A 3-digit number is partitioned into two parts. Both parts are a 2-digit number. What could the 3-digit number and two 2-digit numbers be?
- When reading two 3-digit numbers, the number with the word *thirteen* is greater than the number with the *seventy*. What could the two 3-digit numbers be?
- A 3-digit number has three different digits. Two of the digits are even while the third is odd. If the first digit is smaller than the last two digits, what could the number be?

Rich Tasks

- The post office worker had to calculate the distance for each of his four drivers: Tim, Susie, Adelaide, and Ken. He noticed that each of the workers had to drive a large distance, but that there were significant differences between the amount that some had to drive. In ascending order, arrange the distance each of the workers had to drive. Find the difference between the longest and shortest distance.

- Your class held a fundraiser for the upcoming end-of-year school trip. The number of people attending the fundraiser exceeded expectations. When counting the total money raised, you noticed that there was a lot of paper money. How much money was raised and what was the breakdown of paper money?
- The school received a large donation from a former teacher. When the school cashed the cheque at the bank, the school noticed that they received different kinds of paper bills. There were a lot of $5s, $20s, and $50s, but not many $10s and $100s. How much money was raised and what was the breakdown of paper money?
- A small community started a recycling challenge. Four groups signed up for the challenge. After two months, two of the groups had collected a large number of items, one group collected very little, and the fourth group was somewhere in between. Arrange the number of items in descending order so that the community can announce the results starting with the winner. How many items were collected in total?

Ill-Defined Problems

- A class couldn't decide which activities to do on Fun Day. Their teacher wanted to make a decision that would be fair to everyone, so he came up with a plan.
- The manipulatives in the classroom are a mess. Students are being asked to help organize the manipulatives so that there is a clear inventory and organizational system.

Teacher Moves

Questions:

- What number did you represent? How did you decide on your representation?
- Which number is bigger? How did you determine it was that number?
- What number is smaller? How did you determine it was that number?
- What is the value of the digit in the number?
- How can you break this number into smaller parts?
- Do you still have the same amount when you break it into two smaller parts?

Next Steps:

- If students are not matching the correct quantity to the given number, ensure that they can correctly identify the number.
- If students are having difficulty matching the correct quantity to the given number, ensure that they can accurately apply the counting principles.
- If students cannot break apart numbers, start with small numbers.
- If students are struggling to know that the two parts combined is the whole number, use one set of concrete objects for the whole. Then, as you partition the whole into two parts, emphasize that you are still using the same number of objects, just rearranging them into smaller numbers.

- I find that if students struggle with partitioning numbers, use students as examples for part-part-whole. Then, move to manipulatives. Sometimes the move to pictures is too quick and this can hinder student understanding.
- If students are having difficulty placing a whole number on the number line, determine if it is due to not understanding the magnitude of the whole number, the relationship between whole numbers on the number line, or a spatial sense concern.

Number: Fractions

Be sure to refer to your curriculum for grade-specific expectations

	Brief Overview	*Look Fors*	**Common Misconceptions**
Represent Fractions	<ul><li>A fraction is a number that describes a relationship between a part and a whole.</li><li>Fractional parts are equal-sized portions of one whole.</li><li>**Numerator** represents "part" and **denominator** represents "whole".</li><li>The two numbers (numerator and denominator) should be considered in relation to one another.</li></ul>	<ul><li>Students can represent a given fraction concretely and pictorially.</li><li>Students can record the fraction for a given situation (concretely or pictorially).</li><li>Students can identify, model, and explain the meaning of numerator and denominator.</li><li>Students can identify instances when parts are not equally sized.</li></ul>	<ul><li>Students have confusion regarding numerator and denominator.</li><li>Students think of the two numbers as separate.</li><li>Students are not using equal sized parts.</li><li>Students do not understand the whole.</li></ul>
Compare Fractions	<ul><li>Comparing fractions using concrete and pictorial representations.</li><li>At this level, fractions with like denominators are compared.</li><li>There is a progression in mathematical language.</li><li>Initially, terms such as **more**, **less**, **same**, are acceptable.</li><li>Eventually, move towards **equal**, **greater than** and **less than** when comparing numbers.</li></ul>	<ul><li>Students can compare given fractions with like denominators using models.</li><li>Students use concrete and/or pictorial representations of the fractions.</li></ul>	<ul><li>Students use the wrong symbols (<, >, =).</li><li>Students think of the numbers (numerator and denominator) as two separate numbers.</li></ul>

Problem Types

Procedural Problems

- Represent $\frac{3}{5}$ pictorially.
- Record the fraction for the given pictorial representation:

- Arrange the following fractions in ascending order:

  $\frac{7}{8}$ $\frac{1}{8}$ $\frac{4}{8}$ $\frac{3}{8}$

- Use <, >, or = to compare the following fractions:

  $\frac{2}{4} \bigcirc \frac{3}{4}$

- Circle the representation that does not have equal parts.

Words-as-Labels Problems

- Dom ate $\frac{1}{4}$ of dinner while Tami ate $\frac{2}{4}$ of their dinner. Who ate most of their dinner?
- A family ordered a rectangular cake to share for dessert. The cake was cut into 10 slices. Represent this cake in a drawing.
- The librarian put out eight books for students to read. Three of the books were read. What fraction of the books were read?
- A student was coloring a rectangle divided into parts. What fraction of the rectangle did the student have colored?

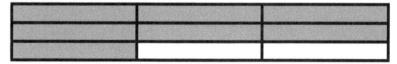

- Three friends decided to paint the fence around their old school. Luis painted $\frac{2}{6}$ of the fence, Helen painted $\frac{3}{6}$ of the fence, and Shelly painted $\frac{1}{6}$ of the fence. Arrange the three friends in ascending order based on how much they painted.

Open-Ended Problems

- How can you divide a circle into equal parts?
- You cut a rectangle into an odd number of equal pieces. Represent some of these pieces as a fraction.
- Each equal part of a circle is colored with one of two colors. What fraction of the circle is colored with each of the two colors?
- Select a small number for the numerator and a larger number for the denominator. Represent this fraction pictorially.
- There are a lot more shaded parts of a rectangle than non-shaded parts. What fraction of the rectangle is shaded?

Rich Tasks

- Mark, Sally, Tia, and Scott volunteered to build four flower boxes for the community park. Each of them finished a different amount of their flower boxes. As a fraction, record the amount of flower box each person finished. Represent each fraction as a visual.
- Duane and Dana decided to work together to build a bench for their old school. Dana did most of the work. Record the amount of work each person did as a fraction. Represent each fraction as a visual.
- Raya brought a bag of marbles to school. There were more than 10 marbles in the bag. The marbles were either red, blue, or green. What fraction of the marbles is red? What fraction of the marbles is blue? What fraction of the marbles is green? Order the colors from greatest to least.
- Three students participated in a trivia challenge. Two students tied with the most questions answered correctly. The third student only answered a few questions correctly. Record a fraction for each student and arrange them in ascending order.

Ill-Defined Problems

- A local restaurant is creating a new menu and would like to know what kind of foods are popular with children. They were hoping we could help by testing some foods with our class and letting them know the fraction of students that liked each food.
- We need to plan a celebration to end our writing unit. Prior to the celebration, we have to plan and determine what portion of people will be bringing the different supplies needed. Let's figure it out.

Teacher Moves

Questions:

- What does that fraction represent?
- What does the numerator mean? What does the denominator mean?
- What would be an example of a fraction that we can see in this class?
- What strategy can you use to compare two fractions?

Next Steps:

- If students are having difficulty understanding the whole, encourage them to circle the whole shape so that they know what the denominator represents.
- If students are thinking of the numerator and denominator as two separate whole numbers, have them draw lines from each to the corresponding aspect in the picture.
- If students are having difficulty applying the < and > symbols, have them use the terminology (less than, greater than) first. Then, use the terminology and record the symbol below the words. Then, move to only using the symbol.
- If students are having difficulty understanding the terms ascending and descending, provide opportunities to connect the terms to the phrases, "from least to greatest" and "from greatest to least."

Number: Addition & Subtraction

*Be sure to refer to your curriculum for grade-specific expectations**

	Brief Overview	*Look Fors*	**Common Misconceptions**
Add and Subtract Whole Numbers (Solve)	• Addition and subtraction involve the ability to: • Solve addition and subtraction problems and • Add and subtract numbers up to 1000 efficiently. • Addition and subtraction should be taught simultaneously so students see the relationship between the two operations.	• Students can solve addition and subtraction expressions concretely, pictorially, and symbolically. • Students can solve addition and subtraction word problems reflective of the four problem structures. • Students can create a word problem for a given number sentence or solution.	• Students are not sure when to add or subtract. • Students make incorrect calculations. • Students have difficulty regrouping. • Students are not aligning digits.
Add and Subtract Whole Numbers (Estimate)	• Estimation is about working with friendly numbers. Encourage students to use the following words and phrases when estimating: about, approximately, between, a little more than, a little less than, close, close to, and near.	• Students can estimate the sum or difference for a given problem (both an expression and a word problem). • Students can use and describe their estimation strategy. • Students can rationalize why their estimate is accurate.	• Students are not making accurate estimates. • Students change their estimate after calculation. • Students confuse estimating with rounding. • Students cannot explain their thinking.
Mental Math: Fact Learning	• Fact learning is strategy-based because facts are clustered within commonalities. • Instant recall of basic facts is fundamental for mental computation. • Quick recall of facts is 3 seconds or less.	• Students can select from various fact-learning strategies to find the most effective and efficient one. • Students can mentally process the facts in their mind in 3 seconds or less. • Students can explain their thinking.	• Students have to count on their fingers. • Students have difficulty recalling subtraction facts (especially if addition facts aren't mastered).

Problem Types

Procedural Problems

- Solve:
    509 – 47
- Solve:
    464 + 372
- Estimate:
    201 + 395

- Estimate:

    903 – 323
- Which estimate is more accurate for 374 + 498?

    700 or 900
- Without paper and pencil, solve:

    6 + 9
- Without paper and pencil, solve:

    12 – 6

Words-as-Labels Problems

- To raise money for a food drive, the local town council hosted a concert. There were 358 adults and 524 children in attendance. How many people attended the concert?
- A hockey team was invited to the provincial capital for an awards show. On the first day, the team traveled 239 km. On the second day, the team traveled 448 km. If the distance to the awards show is 976 km, how much further does the team still have to drive?
- A small town in Ontario had a population of 387 twenty years ago. Since then, the town has grown to include additional areas. Now the population of the town is 864. How many more people are there in the town now than compared to twenty years ago?
- A group of students were given $950 to purchase outdoor supplies for their school. They decided to buy a bench, a garbage can, and a picnic table. How much money do they have left?

Supplies	Price
Bench	$275
Garbage Can	$60
Shed	$495
Picnic Table	$350

- Emerald, Rya, and Gina each have a collection of hockey cards. Emerald has the smallest collection. Rya has 61 more cards than Emerald. Gina has 38 more cards than Rya. Gina has 106 cards in her collection. How many hockey cards does Emerald have in her collection? Show your work.
- Simon went hiking. He hiked 221 km the first week and 298 km the second week. About how many kilometers did Simon hike? Explain your estimate.
- Greg and Jerry decided to bake cookies for a community picnic. Greg baked 691 cookies and Jerry baked 514 cookies. About how many more cookies did Greg bake than Jerry? Explain your estimate.

Open-Ended Problems

- The sum of two 2-digit numbers is a 3-digit number. What could the two 2-digit numbers be?
- The difference between two large numbers is a 3-digit number. What could the two large numbers be?
- The sum of two 3-digit numbers is a 3-digit number. What could the two 3-digit numbers be?

- The estimated difference between two numbers is 80. What could the two numbers be?
- How does knowing what 9 + 4 equals help with solving 13 – 5?

Rich Tasks

- You were asked to estimate the number of items raised at the local food drive. You notice that there were a lot of items donated into the following categories: cereal, soup, bread, and frozen. How many items were donated in each of the four categories and what is the estimated total number of items raised at the food drive?
- A group of three students decided to collect items to be recycled. They set a goal that many thought was too high. Over a four-month period, the students collected many items. Two of the students collected a lot, while the third student collected only a little. How many items were collected by each student? How many more items would they have to collect to reach their goal?
- Students kept track of the weather during the school year. At the end of the year, the students noticed that many of the days were sunny. The second most common weather was rain. There were only a few snow days. Answer the following three questions:
  - How many days was it sunny?
  - How many days was there rain?
  - How many fewer days was there snow than sun?
- The local cycling club decided to enter a marathon. During the first month, the club cycled a lot of kilometers. The second month was a little less. The third month was their best month by a lot of kilometers. How many kilometers did they travel altogether? How many more kilometers did they cycle in the first month than the third month?

Ill-Defined Problems

This question could be as simple as students focusing solely on surveying people to see their preferences, or could include more complex tasks such as students comparing the number of people wanting different options, calculating the numbers for different options, estimating the costs of different trips, calculating the distance, etc. As such this problem will also be listed as an ill-defined problem in the other relevant key concepts.

- We have to start planning our traditional end-of-year event. Our principal wants to know the cost of such an event and would love to have input from everyone in making this decision.
- Our school needs to purchase new equipment for physical education classes. To raise money to pay for the new equipment, they'd like to host various fundraisers throughout the year. What kind of fundraisers should they host and how much do you think each event should make if they want to cover all of the costs of the new equipment?

Teacher Moves

Questions:

- How did you decide whether to add or subtract?
- How did you know that your response was accurate?
- What was your estimation strategy?
- What is the problem asking of you?
- What mental math strategy did you use to solve the problem?

Next Steps:

- If students are having difficulty deciding whether to add or subtract, have them read the problem and think of it as a whole. Do not encourage key words as this is a misleading approach.
- If students are having difficulty recognizing the reasonableness of their response, have them reread the problem once they complete it to see if their response aligns with the other numbers.
- If students are having difficulty applying mental math strategies, take inventory of what strategies they have mastered and then focus on supporting them knowing when to apply such strategies.
- Encourage students to estimate a solution before calculating one. This estimate can be used to self-monitor their work during the calculation.
- If students are having difficulty aligning digits when adding or subtracting, offer grid paper.

Number: Multiplication & Division

Be sure to refer to your curriculum for grade-specific expectations

	Brief Overview	*Look Fors*	**Common Misconceptions**
Multiply and Divide Whole Numbers (Solve)	• Multiplication focuses on **equal groups** and repeated addition. • Division focuses on equal sharing (**partitive**), equal grouping (**quotative**), and repeated subtraction. • Problems are focused on products to 10×10 and related division facts. • Concrete and pictorial models are used to represent the meaning and application of multiplication and division. • Multiplication and division should be taught simultaneously so students see the relationship between the two operations.	• Students can represent a multiplication expression in equal groups, **arrays**, and repeated addition. • Students can represent a division expression in equal groups, equal sharing, and repeated subtraction. • Students can solve a problem, in context, involving multiplication and division. • Students can relate multiplication and division using number sentences. • Students can create a word problem for a given multiplication or division expression.	• Students struggle with 'groups of.' • Students are unsure when to multiply or divide. • Students are unsure what to do with remainders.

Problem Types

Procedural Problems

- Solve 4×8
- Solve $18 \div 2$
- Create a word problem for the following multiplication expression:
    3×9
- Create a word problem for the following division expression:
    $25 \div 5$
- Is the following statement True or False:
    $21 \div 7 = 3$

Words-as-Labels Problems

- Marc drives to work five days a week. Each day he drives 9 kilometers. How many kilometers does Marc drive to work each week?
- Tanya saved six times as much money this week as she saved last week. If Tanya saved $8 last week, how much money did she save this week?
- A group of workers set up 9 rows of chairs with 5 chairs in each row in the gym. How many chairs did they set up?
- Sam bought 16 candies and gave 2 candies to each of his friends. How many friends does Sam have?
- A ping pong tournament was being held at the youth center. Each ping pong game needed four paddles. If the referee bought 24 paddles, how many ping pong games can there be?

Open-Ended Problems

- The product of two numbers is a 2-digit number. What could the two numbers be?
- A large number is divided by a small number. What could the answer be?
- You multiply two numbers and the product is between 20 and 30. What could the two numbers be?
- You have a large number to be divided into small groups. What number did you start with and how many will be in each group?
- The answer to a division problem is between 2 and 10. What could the question be?

Rich Tasks

- There are some bikes outside the school. If you were to count the number of wheels, how many would there be?
- A group of friends like to collect things. Each friend has the same amount of hockey cards in their collection. How many hockey cards are in the friends' collections?
- While preparing for a party, Marcus purchased several balloons. If Marcus wants each person to get the same number of balloons, how many will each receive?
- There were four vans booked to take a group of children to their hockey game. If each van held the same number of children, how many children went to the game and how many were in each van?
- A party planner was designing the seating area for a concert. The planner had to arrange several rows so that each had the same number of chairs. How many chairs would be in each of the rows?

Ill-Defined Problems

- We need to decide on a craft to make as a class. By doing the craft as a class, we will need a few people to bring each of the necessary materials. When you sign up for a material to bring, please indicate how much of the item you will bring. What craft should we make and what amount will we have for each material?
- The librarian just purchased new fiction and non-fiction books at the school's book fair. They need help in determining how to fairly share the books with the primary classes.

Teacher Moves

Questions:

- How did you decide whether to multiply or divide?
- How did you know that your response was accurate?
- What is the problem asking of you?
- Does the representation align with the problem?

Next Steps:

- If students are having difficulty in understanding whether to multiply or divide, model and encourage paraphrasing the problem before attempting to craft a plan. By paraphrasing, students will be checking their understanding of the problem which will lead to making a more informed choice during the planning part of problem-solving.
- Model and encourage students to represent the problem concretely and pictorially before working symbolically. The concrete and pictorial representation can be used to monitor comprehension as students solve it symbolically.

Algebra: Patterns

Be sure to refer to your curriculum for grade-specific expectations

	Brief Overview	Look Fors	Common Misconceptions
Identify and Describe Patterns	• Repeating, increasing, and decreasing patterns consisting of numbers to 1000. • Repeating, increasing, and decreasing patterns consisting of concrete materials, pictures, sounds, and actions. • **Ordinal numbers** (to 100th) are used to refer to or predict terms within a pattern.	• Students can extend repeating patterns. • Students can use a pattern rule (starting point and description of how the pattern continues) to describe and extend an increasing and decreasing pattern. • Students can identify errors in a given pattern. • Students can create a pattern for a given pattern rule.	• Students struggle to identify the pattern rule. • Students struggle to generate a pattern for a given pattern rule. • Students struggle to extend a pattern. • Students are unable to identify errors in a given pattern.

| | | • Students can use ordinal numbers to refer to terms within a pattern. | |
| | | | |

Problem Types

Procedural Problems

- What comes next in the following pattern?
  ✓ ✓ ✗ ✓ ✓ ✗ ✓ ✓ ✗ ✓ ✓ ✗ ✓ ✓ ✗
- What is the pattern rule in the following sequence?
  2, 4, 6, 8, 10, 12
- What is the next number in the sequence?
  0, 3, 6, 9, 12, 15
- Write a number sequence that follows the given pattern rule:
- Start at 90 and decrease by 5
- Identify the error in the following pattern:
  52, 50, 48, 46, 44, 43

Words-as-Labels Problems

- A teacher started with 3 books. On her way through the school, she picked up 2 books from each class. How many books will she have when she leaves the fifth classroom?
- A baker started with 18 cookies in his basket. For each person he visited, he gave away two cookies. How many cookies will he have when he leaves the sixth house?
- There were eighteen students in the class waiting to go to recess. The teacher asked every third student to raise a hand. Represent this repeating pattern using letters.
- There was a collection of new pencils on the table at the art center. Five students went back to the table and each took 2 pencils. There are now 10 pencils left. How many pencils were originally in the collection? What is the pattern rule for this scenario?
- As a classroom reward, students would get to play a math game on every fifth day. Represent this pattern on the following number chart:

1	2	3	4	5	6	7	8	9	10
11	12	13	14	15	16	17	18	19	20
21	22	23	24	25	26	27	28	29	30
31	32	33	34	35	36	37	38	39	40
41	42	43	44	45	46	47	48	49	50
51	52	53	54	55	56	57	58	59	60
61	62	63	64	65	66	67	68	69	70
71	72	73	74	75	76	77	78	79	80
81	82	83	84	85	86	87	88	89	90
91	92	93	94	95	96	97	98	99	100

Open-Ended Problems

- The fourth number in an increasing pattern is 36. What could the first three numbers be?
- The fourth number in a decreasing pattern is 12. What could the first three numbers be?
- Numbers increased by a large amount. What could be the first 5 numbers in the pattern?
- Numbers decreased by a small amount. What could be the first 5 numbers in the pattern?
- There are four elements in a repeating pattern. What could the core of the pattern be?

Rich Tasks

- Marsha started her fundraising drive with a little money. Marsha received the same donation from each house she visited. Write a number sequence for how much she had after each visit. What is the pattern rule?
- Dominique started with a large amount of money to give to charities. If Dominique made the same donation to each charity, how much money does she have left after leaving the fifth charity? Write a number sequence for how much she had after each charity. What is the pattern rule?
- The art class wanted to make a border for the school mural that was just painted in the lobby. They decided to use three different shapes in the border. If they went with a repeating pattern design, how could it be represented in letters?
- The teacher challenged his students to create a pattern that he had to solve. The sixth term in the pattern had to be a number less than 20. What could the pattern be?
- A student recognized errors in a repeating pattern consisting of three elements. What could the errored repeating pattern have been and how could it have been fixed?

Ill-Defined Problems

- We are working with quillwork as part of our multiculturalism unit. The class must decide on what to make and what their quillwork will look like.
- The school has just designated part of the paved area for student play during recess. The principal wants the outline of this area to be artistic and representative of the local community.

Teacher Moves

Questions:

- What is the pattern rule?
- What would come next?
- Can we make that pattern using other items?
- What is the error in this pattern?

Next Steps:

- If students are only offering an incomplete pattern rule (missing either the starting point, size of jump, or direction of jump), perhaps offer a graphic organizer where they have to fill in the three parts of the pattern rule.
- If students cannot apply a pattern rule to generate a pattern, identify what aspect of the rule they are having difficulty with and focus on that. Continue to hone in on this until students can apply all three parts of the pattern rule.
- When replicating patterns, leave the original pattern in place and reproduce it directly below. Students can then match items until their comfort level grows.

Algebra: Solve Equations

Be sure to refer to your curriculum for grade-specific expectations

	Brief Overview	**Look Fors**	**Common Misconceptions**
Solve Equations with Symbols	• An equation is a mathematical statement that includes an equal sign. • The equal sign tells us that the quantity on the left is the same as the quantity on the right. • The concepts of equality and inequality and the meaning of the symbols = and ≠ form the basis of solving equations. • A symbol is used to represent an unknown number in an equation.	• Students can explain the purpose of the symbol in a given equation with one unknown. • Students can solve a given equation using a variety of strategies.	• Students do not understand that the = symbol means equivalence/balance.

Problem Types

Procedural Problems

Be mindful to move the unknown to be on the left and right sides of the equal sign. This will encourage the notion of equality and balance in equations.

When creating sample equations, you can use a question mark (?) for the unknown number, or shapes like I've done in a few examples here.

- Find a number that makes each equation true:

    $9 = \triangle + 5$

    $? = 7 + 3$

    $\bigcirc = 13 - 8$

    $14 = ? - 3$

    $8 = 3 + \triangle$

    $12 = 14 - ?$

    $7 + 9 = ?$

    $? - 5 = 3$

    $5 + 3 = ? - 2$

    $? + 4 = 12 - 6$

Words-as-Labels Problems

- There were eight students playing tag at little recess. Then more children joined them at big recess. There are now 14 children playing tag. How many children joined the game? Write an equation that represents this context and solve.
- There were seven goldfish in the fish tank. Four more goldfish were put in the fish tank. How many goldfish are now in the fish tank? Write an equation that represents this context and solve.
- The Grade 3 class had a collection of chapter books. The teacher bought six new chapter books for the collection. Now there are 14 books in the collection. How many chapter books did the Grade 3 class have before the teacher bought more? Write an equation that represents this context and solve.
- The chairs in library are red or green. There are 14 chairs. Six of them are red. How many of the chairs are green? Write an equation that represents this context and solve.
- Josh scored three fewer goals than Julia in the soccer game. Julia scored 12 goals. How many goals did Josh score? Write an equation that represents this context and solve.

Open-Ended Problems

- Create an equation in which the unknown number is small.
- Create an equation in which the unknown number is large.
- Create a word problem for an equation with an unknown number of 8.
- Create an equation that has an addition symbol, the number 13, a number of your choice, and an unknown number (represented by ?).
- Create an equation that has an addition symbol and a subtraction sign, the number 4, two numbers of your choice, and an unknown number (represented by ?).

Rich Tasks

- A group of friends showed up to play a game of soccer. There were less than 12 people on one team. The other team had more players, but decided to bench some players so that the two teams would be even. Write an equation for this scenario using a ? to represent the number of players that were benched.
- Mira and Jax each created an equation with an unknown number (represented by ?). When talking about their equations, both shared that the ? represented the number 7. Mira and Jax assumed that their equations had to be the same. Is this true? Explain your thinking.
- A teacher posted the following information about an equation on chart paper:
  - An unknown number (represented by a ?) is on one side of the equal sign.
  - There is a sum on each side of the equal sign.
  - No numbers repeat.

  What could be the equation?
- A teacher posted the following information about an equation on chart paper:
  - An unknown number (represented by a ?) is on one side of the equal sign.

- There is a product on one side of the equal sign and a sum on the other side of the equal sign.
- No numbers repeat.

What could be the equation?

- Your class is working on addition and subtraction. You decide to make an equation that will have addition on one side of the equal sign and subtraction on the other side of the equal sign. You then decide where you want to put the unknown number (represented by ?). What is your equation?

Ill-Defined Problems

Ill-defined problems are not typically applied to this particular key concept. However, students may engage in solving equations with symbols as they work through ill-defined problems for other key concepts.

Teacher Moves

Questions:

- What does the <u>symbol representing unknown number</u> mean in this equation?
- What does the = symbol represent in this equation?

Next Steps:

- If students cannot identify the unknown number, first check to see if they understand the meaning of the = symbol (equivalence/balance).
- If students cannot identify the unknown, use blocks, an opaque bag (for the unknown number or blocks), and a balance scale. This concrete representation will assist students in understanding equations.

Spatial Sense: Measurement

Be sure to refer to your curriculum for grade-specific expectations

	Brief Overview	*Look Fors*	**Common Misconceptions**
Find the Length	• Measuring the length of an object is a progression from non-standard to standard units. • Non-standard units: Smaller items are used to measure the length of an object, e.g., how many jellybeans long. • Standard units: Length is measured with a single unit as a measuring device, e.g., centimeters and meters.	• Students can estimate the length of an object (in centimeters and meters) using personal referents. • Students can determine and record the length and width of a given 2-D shape. • Students can determine and record the length, width, or height of a given 3-D object.	• Students are unable to iterate (repeat a single unit) to determine measurement. • Students have difficulty in placing the ruler next to the object when measuring length. • Students have difficulty identifying measurement.

		Students can draw a line segment of a given length using a ruler.	
Find the Perimeter	• **Perimeter** is the distance around a shape (measured in standard units).	• Students can find the perimeter of a given regular shape and explain the strategy used. • Students can find the perimeter of a given irregular or composite shape and explain the strategy used. • Students can construct more than one shape for a given perimeter.	• Students are unable to account for all sides of the shape when finding the perimeter. • Students are unable to measure accurately.

Problem Types

Procedural Problems

- Draw a line with a length of 26 cm.
- Provide students with a ruler to measure the length of a pencil.
- Provide students with a photograph and have them measure the length and width of the picture.
- Ask students to measure the length of an item without using zero as the starting point.
- Find the perimeter of a square with a side length of 32 cm.
- Find the perimeter of the following shape:

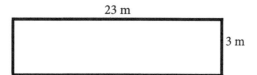

23 m

3 m

Words-as-Labels Problems

- Students were selecting shapes to use as part of a classroom design. They needed shapes that had a length less than 13 cm. Could they use the following shape? Explain your thinking.

- Sully wanted to mail pictures to a friend. When at the post office, Sully was told that he could only mail pictures that were less than 30 cm. He had two pictures that he wanted to send. Can he send both? Explain your thinking.

A

B

- A rectangular bulletin board was put up outside of the local art studio. What is the perimeter of this bulletin board if the width is 125 cm and the length is 400 cm?
- Community members are building a dog park. This space is being planned to hold 14 dogs at any one time and it will be four-sided. If the perimeter is 208 m and if three of the sides are as shown below, what is the length of the fourth side?

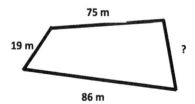

- The school designed a new outdoor play area for students. The space was quite large as there were many students wanting to play in it. The rectangular play area has a length of 78 meters and a width of 36 meters. What is the perimeter of this outdoor play area?

Open-Ended Problems

- Draw two line-segments that are close in measurement. What is the length of each line?
- One line segment is much longer than the other line segment. What is the length of each line?
- The perimeter of a quadrilateral is 84 m. What are the lengths of each side?
- Two of the sides on a shape are much longer than the other two sides. What could the perimeter be?
- The perimeter of a triangle was the same as the perimeter of a rectangle. What could the side lengths be for each shape?

Rich Tasks

- My ruler was broken. When I lined the ruler up next to a book cover, I saw 48 cm next to the bottom of the book cover. What could the length of the book be? What number was next to the top of the book cover?
- Two students were asked to draw a line segment. When the teacher compared the two lines, she noticed that both lines were the same length. One student said that the number on the ruler at the end of her line was 12. The other student said that the number on the ruler at the end of his line was 24. Both students measured correctly. How is this possible that their numbers differed?
- Students were asked to measure the length of a basketball rim. Some students said that it couldn't be done as it was curved. Other students said that it could be done. Who do you agree with? Explain your thinking.
- Students were challenged to design a garden space for the school science club. Of the three spaces that were designed, two had a large perimeter while the third space had a much smaller perimeter. Draw the three garden spaces and be sure to label the lengths of each side. What is the perimeter of each space?
- Two carpenters went to a building supply store to ask for fencing. Both carpenters constructed new bike parking pads. One carpenter constructed a parking pad for a school while the other carpenter constructed a parking

pad for the community center's scooters. While each carpenter needed the same amount of fencing, the shape of their parking pads was different. What could be the perimeter of the two parking pads? What could the side lengths be for each of the parking pads?

Ill-Defined Problems

- Our school was selected as the site for the cross-country meet and has to decide on and plan how they would accommodate people wanting to attend.
- There needs to be a new basketball space on the playground designated for primary students. We are being asked to come together and determine the best design so that basketballs won't roll out of the area.

This question could be as simple as students focusing solely on identifying the number of people that may attend, or could include more complex tasks such as surveying people to see how many should attend, designing a space to accommodate attendees, counting the number of attendees, and then partitioning them along the site, etc. As such, this problem will also be listed as an ill-defined problem under other relevant key concepts.

Teacher Moves

Questions:

- What is length of this shape? How did you determine this?
- How do you use a ruler?
- What does perimeter mean?

Next Steps:

- If using non-standard units to determine a length, students may need to iterate the unit being used to measure if there is only one of it. Model this iteration using multiple items.
- If students are having difficulty using a ruler, provide them with a broken ruler. This will require students to focus on the main principles of using a ruler to measure length.
- If students are having difficulty determining the perimeter, encourage them to make a mark on the sides they have measured or included in the formula so that they don't forget to include it in the measurement or so that they don't double count a side.

Data: Data Management

Be sure to refer to your curriculum for grade-specific expectations

	Brief Overview	*Look Fors*	**Common Misconceptions**
Collect, Record, Organize, and Analyze Data	• Collecting, organizing, and displaying data in a meaningful way.	• Students can collect and record data. • Students can organize data using tally marks, lists, charts, line plots, and bar graphs. • Students can answer questions related to a given line plot, chart, bar graph, or list.	• Students are unable to accurately record data. • Students are unable to organize data. • Students are unable to accurately display data. • Students are unable to analyze data.

Problem Types

Procedural Problems

- Read the data within the table:

Favorite Colors	
Colors	**Number of Children**
Red	||||| ||||
Green	||||| ||||| |||
Orange	|||||
Blue	||||| ||||
Pink	||||| ||

How many children choose red as their favorite color?
How many children choose blue as their favorite color?
What color was the least favorite?
How many children were asked about their favorite color?
What colors were selected by the same number of children?

- Organize the following data into a chart.

<u>Favorite Vegetable</u>
Corn ||||| ||
Cucumber ||||| |||||
Broccoli ||||
Lettuce |

- Create a line plot for the following data:

<u>Number of Siblings</u>
Zero ||||| |||
One ||||| ||||| ||
Two |||
Three
Four ||

- Create a line plot using the same data as shown in the bar graph below.

Favourite Sports

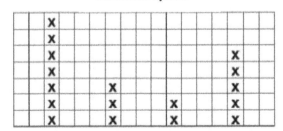

Hockey   Football   Soccer   Tennis

Words-as-Labels Problems

- A teacher wanted to find out how many students consider winter to be their favorite season. After asking all of the Kindergarten to Grade 6 students, the teacher listed the results in a table:

Grade	Number of Students
K	13
1	8
2	9
3	10
4	10
5	11
6	8

Draw a bar graph.

Which grade saw the least number of students choose winter as their favorite season?

- The community council wanted to start a youth sports league. First, they decided to interview some children about their favorite sport.

Favourite Sports

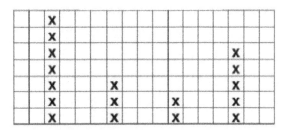

Hockey   Football   Soccer   Tennis

- How many more students like tennis than soccer?
- How many children were asked for their favorite sport?
- Which sport is the least popular?
- Which sport is the most popular?
- A group of retired people were asked about their favorite hobby. How many people were asked? What hobby was selected by 9 retired people as being their favorite?

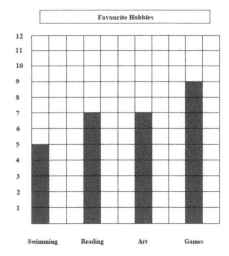

Open-Ended Problems

- What question could you write if you were interested in finding out about students and the sports they play?
- Create a bar graph that answers a question about food.
- Create a line plot where two items have the same number.
- What questions could you ask someone to check if they understood the following graph?

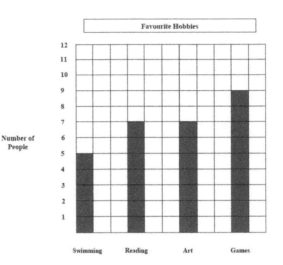

Rich Tasks

- A teacher asks her students what they ate for lunch. After the data is collected, you notice that there is quite a difference in the responses for certain foods. Create a bar graph that would represent such a data set and include two questions that you would like others to answer about your graph.
- You are provided the following frequency table that is only partially completed:

Preferred _____		
	Tally	**Number**
		8
	＋＋＋＋ ＋＋＋＋	
Flying		7
		12

Decide on a way to share this data so that others will understand what the data means. Be sure to include two questions that you can ask others about the data as a way to check for understanding.

- You have been assigned a role on the school newspaper. As part of this role, you are asked to design a survey, record collected data, and graph the findings. Your data will then be displayed in the newspaper for all students and teachers to see. The only rule you are given is that the data must relate to school.

The first question could be as simple as students focusing solely on identifying the number of people that may attend, or could include more complex tasks such as surveying people to see how many should attend, designing a space to accommodate attendees, counting the number of attendees, and then partitioning them along the site, etc. As such, this problem will also be listed as an ill-defined problem under other relevant key concepts.

The second question could be as simple as students focusing solely on surveying people to see their preferences, or could include more complex tasks such as students comparing the number of people wanting different options, calculating the numbers for different options, estimating the costs of different trips, calculating the distance, etc. As such, this problem will also be listed as an ill-defined problem under other relevant key concepts.

Ill-Defined Problems

- Our school was selected as the site for the cross-country meet and has to decide on and plan how they would accommodate people wanting to attend.
- We have to start planning our traditional end-of-year event. Our principal wants to know the cost of such an event and would love to have input from everyone in making this decision.

Teacher Moves

Questions:

- What are you collecting data on? What is your question? How are you organizing the data?
- How will you display the data?
- What is the data telling us?

Next Steps:

- If students are having difficulty recording and organizing data, offer them a graphic organizer to assist in the process. Over time, you may remove this graphic organizer if students are demonstrating progress.
- If students are forgetting aspects in constructing the plot/chart/graph/list, provide a checklist of the steps so that they can apply them one-by-one. Over time, you may remove this checklist if students are demonstrating progress.
- If students are having difficulty analyzing data, offer them literal questions. Once students can demonstrate success answering literal questions, move to more analytical questions. Model and encourage students to talk through their thinking as they answer the question.

Financial Literacy: Money Concepts

Be sure to refer to your curriculum for grade-specific expectations

	Brief Overview	*Look Fors*	**Common Misconceptions**
Identify Different Ways to Represent Amounts of Money	• The understanding of money. • There are various ways to represent the same amount of money. • Financial literacy provides real-life context for calculations and estimation.	• Students can represent an amount of money in a variety of ways.	• Students do not understand the individual value of bills and coins. • Students inaccurately add coins and bills when trying to represent the given amount of money.

Problem Types

Procedural Problems

- Represent $95 in bills.
- Represent 40¢ in coins.
- Determine two ways to represent $70 with paper money.
- Determine two ways to represent 85¢ in coins.
- What value does the following represent:

  4 dimes, 1 nickel, 1 quarter

Words-as-Labels Problems

- Talia bought a new book for the cost of $17. Talia wants to pay in cash without getting change back. What combination of paper money could Talia use to do this?
- David went to the bank with a collection of bills that totaled $50. He had the most amount of bills that could possibly total $50. What bills did David take to the bank?
- There was a pile of coins on the countertop. When the worker looked through the pile, he noticed the following coins:

  1 dime, 3 nickels, 2 quarters
- A new soccer ball costs $37. Simon has the following in paper money in his wallet:

  $10, $5, $10, $5

  Does Simon have enough money to pay for the soccer ball?
- Anita went to the bank with a collection of coins that totaled 80¢. She had the least number of coins that could possibly total 80¢. What coins did Anita take to the bank?

Open-Ended Problems

- Represent a dollar amount using seven bills.
- Represent a dollar amount using four coins.
- Represent $95 with an amount of paper money.
- Represent 55¢ with a number of coins.
- You have a collection of bills that are all different. What is the value of all these bills?

Rich Tasks

- On your way to school, you notice that you have a collection of coins in your pocket. There are nickels, dimes, and quarters. You have between 90 cents and one dollar. What coins could you have?
- When you were counting all your coins, many of them fell off the desk. You grabbed a handful of coins off the floor. What coins did you grab and what is the dollar value of these coins?
- When you were counting all your paper money, some fell off the desk. You picked this paper money off the floor. What paper money fell to the floor and what is the total value of this paper money?
- Two students say that they have the same amount of money in their pocket. Can both students have the same amount of money if one has a lot of bills in his pocket and one doesn't have many bills in his pocket? Explain your thinking.

- Two students say that they have different amounts of money in their pocket but they each have the same number of coins. Can both students have different amounts of money in their pockets but different amounts of coins? Explain your thinking.

Ill-Defined Problems

- Authors use a lot of different tools when creating a text. We need to buy more of these tools, but we know that we have limited space in the writing center and we have a limited budget. We need to decide on which items would be most used by students.
- We have to start planning our traditional end-of-year event. Our principal wants to know the cost of such an event and would love to have input from everyone in making this decision.

The first question could be as simple as students focusing solely on counting items for the treat bags, or could include more complex tasks such as students deciding which items to include, how many of the items, the costs associated with the items, etc. As such, this problem will also be listed as an ill-defined problem under other relevant key concepts.

The second question could be as simple as students focusing solely on surveying people to see their preferences, or could include more complex tasks such as students comparing the number of people wanting different options, calculating the numbers for different options, estimating the costs of different trips, calculating the distance, etc. As such, this problem will also be listed as an ill-defined problem under other relevant key concepts.

Teacher Moves

Questions:

- What are the values of coins and paper money?
- What dollar value are you representing?
- Why did you decide to represent the dollar amount the way you did?

Next Steps:

- If students are having difficulty with the values of coins and paper money, offer visuals that will assist them in learning and remembering the values.
- If students are misrepresenting a given money value, take note if it is an addition/subtraction issue or a misunderstanding of the values of coins and paper money.

5

Elementary (Grades 4–6)

This chapter covers the key concepts used in the Elementary level (Grades 4–6). As stated in Chapter 1, the concepts are categorized by strand. Within each strand, I have clustered key concepts within central ideas so that teachers can easily sift through this resource to identify problems that address a range of learning needs in the classroom. For example, I've categorized whole numbers as its own group, and list all the relevant key concepts for it. I also have categorized other groups (decimals, fractions, integers, equations, measurement, etc.), and list all the relevant key concepts for each.

For each key concept, I provide a brief overview of the concept, *look fors*, and common misconceptions. In addition, I also provide a suggestion as to where in the lesson such problems may fit (i.e., warm-up, independent practice, consolidation).

Elementary Key Concepts	
Number	**Whole Numbers** • Represent Numbers • Partition Numbers • Compare Numbers • Place Value **Decimals** • Represent Numbers • Partition Numbers • Compare Numbers • Place Value **Fractions** • Represent Fractions • Compare Fractions

Number	**Relate Numbers**
	• Relate Fractions, Decimal Numbers, and Percent
	
	Integers
	• Represent Integers
	• Compare Integers
	
	Addition & Subtraction
	• Add and Subtract Whole Numbers
	  • Solve
	  • Estimate
	• Add and Subtract Decimal Numbers
	  • Solve
	  • Estimate
	
	Multiplication & Division
	• Multiply and Divide Whole Numbers
	  • Solve
	  • Estimate
	• Multiply and Divide Decimal Numbers
	  • Solve
	  • Estimate
	• Mental Math: Fact Learning	

Algebra (Patterns & Relations)	**Solve Equations** • Solve Equations with Variables	
Spatial Sense (Shape & Space)	**Measurement** • Find the Perimeter, Area, and Volume **Geometry** • Measure Angles	
Data (Statistics & Probability)	**Data Management** • Collect, Record, Organize, and Analyze Data Using Graphs	
Financial Literacy	**Cost of Transactions** • Estimate and Calculate Cost of Transactions	

This chapter is meant to be practical, so that educators can strengthen their understanding of the key concepts and have a large number of problems that they can bring into the classroom. These problems will be reflective of the different problem types explained in Chapter 2. Please note, however, that not all key concepts align with all problem types. I highlight any omissions throughout this chapter.

When considering problem types for the elementary level (Grades 4–6), please take note:

- **Procedural problems** can be used throughout a math lesson. At the elementary level, teachers typically use them during teacher-led individual or small-group sessions, math interviews, and independent practice.
- **Words-as-labels problems** can be used for warm-up, math centers, and individual or small-group sessions. More and more, teachers are relying on this problem type to consolidate learning.
- **Open-ended problems** can be used throughout a lesson and are great for differentiation. They can also be used to launch a lesson, provide structure for math centers, and generate discourse during consolidation.
- **Rich tasks** are typically used during the independent part of a lesson. This problem type provides a great opportunity for students to engage with a concept for a duration of time. Much of the work done within rich tasks form the basis of the consolidation block.
- **Ill-defined problems** form the basis of the independent part of a lesson. Similar to rich tasks, this problem type provides a great opportunity for students to engage with a concept for an extended period of time. The thinking done with ill-defined problems forms the basis of the consolidation block.

After each key concept, you'll find suggested teacher moves to aid students in developing their problem-solving abilities and next steps.

Number: Whole Numbers

Be sure to refer to your curriculum for grade-specific expectations

	Brief Overview	*Look Fors*	**Common Misconceptions**
Represent Numbers	• Numbers can be represented in five ways: contextually, concretely, pictorially, symbolically, and verbally.	• Students can read a given number. • Students can write a given number in words. • Students can provide examples of large numbers in print or electronic media. • Students can represent a given number in a variety of ways and explain how they are equivalent. • Students can represent a given number using expressions. • Students can translate between and among different representations.	• Students misrepresent the number. • Students are unable to convert between different representations.

Partition Numbers	• The ability to recognize that any number can be partitioned into two or more smaller numbers.	• Students can show a given number (whole) as two or more parts and name each part. • Students can identify a number (whole) that is represented in two or more parts. • Students recognize that partitioning a number (whole) into two or more parts does not affect the count. • Students can represent the given number as an expression.	• Students do not accurately break the whole into parts. • Students are not confident that the total remains unchanged when broken into parts.
Compare Numbers	• Comparing and ordering numbers. • Comparison of numbers is a process that moves from concrete to pictorial to symbolic representations. • It is important to use mathematical language (equal to, greater than, less than) when comparing numbers.	• Students can compare numbers using pictures, number lines (finding two or more numbers on a number line), benchmarks, and comparing digits (left to right). • Students can order a set of numbers in **ascending** and **descending** order. • Students can justify their solutions.	• Students use the wrong symbols (<, >, =). • Students order numbers the wrong way (ascend/descend). • Students inaccurately place numbers on the number line.

Place Value	• Place value is a system that explains the value of a digit based on its position in the number.
	• Place value is based on the following principles:
	  • Ten digits (0 to 9).
	  • Each place is ten times the value of the place to the right.
	• A number has different forms. 135 is 1 hundred, 3 tens, 5 ones, and is also 13 tens and 5 ones.
	• Zero is a place holder.
		• Students can represent a given number using base-ten blocks.
		• Students can identify a number based on base-ten blocks.
		• Students can represent a given number, in at least two ways, using base-ten blocks.
		• Students can identify the value of a digit in a given number.
		• Students can convert a number between standard form, expanded form, and word form.
			• Students use face value with numbers not place value (instead of recognizing that the 7 in 783 represents 700, they assume it represents 7).
			• Students have difficulty in converting between word, expanded, and standard form.

Problem Types

Procedural Problems

- Represent 1833 in base-ten blocks.
- Write the following number in standard form:
  600 + 8000 + 9
- Record the value of the underlined digit:
  74<u>6</u>2
- Write the following number in expanded form:
  3674
- Order the following numbers in descending order:
  6573, 7365, 6537, 7653, 7536
- Use <, >, or = to compare the following numbers:
  4 502 424 ◯ 4 520 442
- Represent the following number as an expression:
  3484

Words-as-Labels Problems

- The school librarian ordered new books for the library. There were 1362 fiction books and 2423 non-fiction books. How many books were there altogether?
- While reading a book, two students noticed the number 369 081. Both students recorded an expression for this number. One of the students wrote 278 973 + 90 108 while the second student wrote 330 245 + 37 836. Do both expressions equate the number the students noticed in the book?
- While playing a game, Sam rolled the following seven numbers: 3, 8, 9, 0, 5, 3, 6. What is the largest number Sam could make with these numbers? What is the smallest number Sam could make with these numbers?
- The population of four cities is recorded in the table below. Arrange the cities, based on their population, in descending order.

City	Population
Calgary	1 019 942
Mississauga	668 549
Winnipeg	632 063
Vancouver	1 837 969

- A touring company was in business for more than 10 years. During this time, the company used two buses to take travellers across the country. Their 47-passenger bus had an odometer reading 87 983 kilometers. Their 57-passenger bus had an odometer reading 108 937 kilometers. Which bus had travelled more kilometers? What is the difference in the number of kilometers each bus travelled?

Open-Ended Problems

- Use an open number line to place three large numbers. Two of the numbers are much larger than the other number.
- Represent a number using 9 base-ten blocks. Write the number in words.
- Record a 6-digit number that meets the following parameters:

- The digit in the tens place is greater than the digit in the thousands place.
- There is an odd number in the hundred thousands place.
- The digit 7 has a value of 70 000.
- A 5-digit number is partitioned into two parts. Both parts are 4-digit numbers. What could the 5-digit number and two 4-digit numbers be?
- When reading two 6-digit numbers, the number with the word *thirteen* is greater than the number with the word *seventy-eight*. What could the two 6-digit numbers be?
- A five-digit number has three different digits. Two of the digits are even while one digit is odd. If the first digit in the number is smaller than the last two digits in the number, what could the five-digit number be?

Rich Tasks

- The post office worker had to calculate the yearly distance travelled for each of his four drivers: Tim, Susie, Adelaide, and Ken. He noticed that each of the workers had driven distances greater than 100 000 kilometers. While each driver travelled a large distance, there were significant differences between the amount that some had to drive. In ascending order, arrange the distance each of the workers had to drive. Find the difference between the longest and shortest distance.
- Over a two-year period, the local community center ran a fundraiser to help cover the cost of building an extension. The center met their fundraising goal of a six-digit dollar amount. Now, the center needs to decide how much of the money goes to the three different contractors. Create a plan that documents how much of the fundraised money is to go to each of the three contractors.
- The city council decided to start a city-wide recycling challenge. There were four different charities that signed up for the challenge. After the first year, two of the groups had collected a large number of items, one group collected very little, and the fourth group was somewhere in between. In total, the number of items collected was in the six-digit range. Arrange the number of items in descending order so that the city can announce the results. How many items were collected in total?
- You and the other two students in your math group created a new game to play. Before sharing the game with their class, the group decided to play it themselves. One member of the group created a spinner divided into 10 equal sections numbered 0 to 9. Once the spinner was finished, another student spun the spinner six times. Each group member created a number using all 6 digits when spun. What were their three numbers if the group members noticed the following?
  - Two of the numbers had the same digit in the hundreds place.
  - One number was a lot lower than the other two numbers.
  - The sum of all three numbers was still a six-digit number.

Ill-Defined Problems

- The population of our country has seen considerable growth over the years; however, this growth hasn't been consistent from year-to-year.
- Students have been using YouTube videos to support classroom learning. The teacher wants us to create a rating scale based on the number of views.

Teacher Moves

Questions:

- What number did you represent? How did you decide on your representation?
- Which number is bigger? How did you determine it was that number?
- What number is smaller? How did you determine it was that number?
- What is the value of the digit in the number?
- How can you break this number into smaller parts?
- Do you still have the same amount when you break it into two smaller parts?

Next Steps:

- If students are not matching the correct quantity to the given number, ensure that they can correctly identify the number.
- If students are having difficulty matching the correct quantity to the given number, ensure that they can accurately apply the counting principles.
- If students cannot break apart numbers, start with small numbers.
- If students are struggling to know that the two parts combined is the whole number, use one set of concrete objects for the whole. Then, as you partition the whole into two parts, emphasize that you are still using the same number of objects just rearranging them into smaller numbers.
- I find that if students struggle with partitioning numbers symbolically, revert to using manipulatives. Then move to pictures. Sometimes students move too quickly to symbols and this can hinder student understanding.
- If students are having difficulty placing a whole number on the number line, determine if it is due to not understanding the magnitude of the whole number, the relationship between whole numbers on the number line, or a spatial sense concern.

Number: Decimals

Be sure to refer to your curriculum for grade-specific expectations

	Brief Overview	*Look Fors*	**Common Misconceptions**
Represent Numbers	• Numbers can be represented in five ways: contextually, concretely, pictorially, symbolically, and verbally.	• Students can read and write a given decimal. • Students can write the decimal for a given concrete or pictorial representation and vice versa. • Students can represent a given decimal using money values and vice versa. • Students can provide examples of decimals in everyday context.	• Students misrepresent the decimal. • Students are unable to convert between different representations.

		• Students can represent a given decimal using expressions. • Students can identify equivalent decimals.	
Partition Numbers	• The ability to recognize that any number can be partitioned into two or more smaller numbers.	• Students can show a given decimal number (whole) as two or more parts and name each part. • Students can identify a decimal number (whole) that is represented in two or more parts. • Students recognize that partitioning a decimal number (whole) into two or more parts does not affect the whole. • Students can represent the given decimal number (whole) as an expression.	• Students do not accurately break the whole into parts. • Students are not confident that the total remains unchanged when broken into parts.
Compare Numbers	• Comparing and ordering numbers. • Comparison of numbers is a process that moves from concrete, to pictorial, to symbolic representations. • It is important to use mathematical language (equal to, greater than, less than) when comparing numbers.	• Students can compare decimal numbers using pictures, number lines (two or more numbers on a number line), benchmarks, and comparing digits (left-to-right). • Students can order a set of decimal numbers in **ascending** and **descending** order. • Students can justify their solutions.	Students use the wrong symbols ($<$, $>$, $=$). • Students order numbers the wrong way (ascend/ descend). • Students inaccurately place numbers on the number line.
Place Value	• Place value is a system that explains the value of a digit based on its position in the number. • Decimals are an extension in place value of whole numbers. • Place value is based on the following principles: • Ten digits (0 to 9).	• Students can represent a given decimal number using base-ten blocks. • Students can identify a decimal number based on base-ten blocks. • Students can represent a given number, in at least two ways, using base-ten blocks.	• Students use face value with numbers not place value (instead of recognizing that the 7 in 78.3 represents 70, they assume it represents 7). • Students have difficulty in converting between word, expanded, and standard form.

Place Value	• Each place is ten times the value of the place to the right. • A number has different forms. 135 is 1 hundred, 3 tens, 5 ones, and is also 13 tens and 5 ones. • Zero is a place holder.	• Students can identify the value of a digit in a decimal number. • Students can convert a decimal number between standard form, expanded form, and word form.	

Problem Types

Procedural Problems

- Represent 3.29 in base-ten blocks.
- Write the following number in standard form:
  0.08 + 0.9 + 7
- Record the value of the underlined digit:
  82.1$\underline{7}$4
- Write the following number in expanded form:
  535.05
- Order the following numbers in descending order:
  6.204, 6.240, 6, 6.420, 6.402
- Use <, >, or = to compare the following fractions:
  15.02 ○ 15
- Represent the following number as an expression:
  54.39

Words-as-Labels Problems

- Tai bought a new book for a cost of $17.89. Tai only has a $20 bill on her. How much change will Tai get back when paying for the book?
- A carpenter had $10.57 on him. When he looked through the money, he noticed that he had a $10 bill and the rest were coins. What coins could the carpenter have had on him?
- The property values of four historic homes are recorded in the table below. Arrange the homes, based on their property value, in ascending order.

Home	Property Value
Main Street Manor	$944 942.75
Whispering Meadows	$668 549.46
Shady Grove	$1 732 063.35
Magnolia Manor	$1 337 969.53

- A concert hall was in business for ten years. During the first five years of business, the concert hall made a profit of $51 097.43. During the last five years, the concert hall's profit was $104 003.32. How much more was the profit in the last five years than the first five years?

- The school drama club ordered new fabrics for costumes. There were 14.34 meters of red fabric and 24.323 meters of green fabric. What is the total length of all the fabric that was ordered?

Open-Ended Problems

- Use an open number line to place three decimal numbers. Two of the decimal numbers are much smaller than the other decimal number.
- Represent a decimal number using 5 base-ten blocks. Write the number in words.
- Record a decimal number that means the following parameters:
  - The digit in the tens place is greater than the digit in the hundreds place.
  - There is an odd number in the tenths place.
  - The digit 7 has a value of 0.07.
  - There are two digits to the left of the decimal.
- A decimal number is partitioned into two parts. Both parts have three digits to the left of the decimal and two digits to the right of the decimal. What could the decimal number and its two parts be?
- When reading two decimal numbers, the number with the word *seventy-one* is smaller than the number with the word *two*. What could the two decimal numbers be?
- A decimal number has four different digits. Three of the digits are even while one digit is odd. If the first digit in the number is smaller than the last two digits in the number, what could the decimal number be?

Rich Tasks

- Tim, Tammy, Sue, and Jacques are student athletes who ran the 100-meter sprint. While each athlete ran the race in under 20 seconds (each time including a decimal), there were significant differences between the amount of time for some of them. In ascending order, arrange the times of each student athlete. Find the difference in time between the fastest and slowest athlete.
- You and two friends were in a math center together. For that math center, students had to write a 7-digit decimal number. Students had to spin a spinner divided into 10 equal sections with digits 0 to 9. Whatever digit the spinner stopped on, students had to record that digit as part of their 7-digit decimal number. This was then repeated six additional times to complete the number. What were each students' number if they noticed the following:
  - Two of the decimal numbers had the same digit in the hundredths place.
  - One decimal number was a lot lower than the other two numbers.
  - The sum of all three decimal numbers was still a whole number.
- Students were looking over the student council budgets for the past four years. For three of the four years, the council made profits of greater than $1000. For the fourth year, the profit was slightly less than $1000. The profits for each of the four years had two things in common:
  - The numbers to the right of the decimal were less than 75 for three of the four years.
  - There was a digit '4' in each number.

  Record the four profits in ascending order.

- Three students took part in the school's track and field long jump. All three students made it into provincials. Each jump had a distance recorded in meters and consisted of digits to the right of the decimal. The coach wanted to display these three measurements onto a number line to show students how all three jumps were close. Place the three distances onto a number line.

Ill-Defined Problems

- Ads are constantly interrupting our digital experience. Consider how you listen, watch, and consume entertainment, and the length of time of such ads. How does the length of ads compare within the various types of media?
- Our school is raising money for a local charity. Students and staff want to have a successful fundraiser. The principal is looking for help in planning this fundraiser. Specifically, the principal would like to know what new items could be asked for as donations and how much these items would be worth if purchased new.

Teacher Moves

Questions:

- What number did you represent? How did you decide on your representation?
- How did you account for the decimal places in the representation?
- Which number is bigger? How did you determine it was that number?
- What number is smaller? How did you determine it was that number?
- What is the value of the digit in the number?
- How can you break this number into smaller parts?
- Do you still have the same amount when you break it into two smaller parts?
- Do you find it more challenging to work with decimal numbers than whole numbers?

Next Steps:

- If students are not matching the correct quantity to the given number, ensure that they can correctly identify the number.
- If students are having difficulty matching the correct quantity to the given number, ensure that they can accurately apply the counting principles.
- If students are having difficulty in working with decimal numbers, assess if it is solely due to not understanding parts of the unit and digits to the right of the decimal.
- If students cannot break apart numbers, start with small numbers.
- If students are struggling to know that two parts combined is a whole number, use one set of concrete objects for the whole. Then, as you partition the whole into two parts, emphasize that you are still using the same number of objects just rearranging them into smaller numbers.
- I find that if students struggle with partitioning numbers symbolically, revert to using manipulatives. Then move to pictures. Sometimes students move too quickly to symbols and this can hinder student understanding.
- If students are having difficulty placing a decimal number on the number line, determine if it is due to not understanding the magnitude of the decimal number, the relationship between decimal numbers on the number line or a spatial sense concern.

Number: Fractions

Be sure to refer to your curriculum for grade-specific expectations

	Brief Overview	*Look Fors*	**Common Misconceptions**

Represent Fractions	• A fraction is a number that describes a relationship between a part and a whole.
	  • Fractional parts are equal-sized portions of one whole.
	  • **Numerator** represents part and **denominator** represents whole.
	  • The numerator and denominator should be considered in relation to one another.
	• Needs to concretely, pictorially, and symbolically be able to represent fractions.
	• When exploring equivalent fractions, it is encouraged to use concrete and pictorial representations to develop understanding.
	• Improper fractions are fractions greater than one. Improper fractions can be represented as mixed numbers and vice versa.
		• Students can represent a given fraction concretely or pictorially.
		• Students can record the fraction for a given situation (concretely or pictorially).
		• Students can create a set of equivalent fractions and explain why many equivalent fractions exist for any fraction.
		• Students can convert improper fractions to mixed numbers and vice versa.
			• Students have confusion regarding numerator and denominator.
			• Students think of two numbers as separate.
			• Students are not using equal sized parts.
			• Students do not understand the whole.
			• Students have difficulty placing fractions on a number line.
			• Students have difficulty understanding fractions greater than one.

Compare Fractions	• Comparing and ordering fractions involves concrete and pictorial representations.
	• It is important to use mathematical language (**equal to, greater than, less than**) when comparing fractions.
		• Students can compare fractions by:
		  • Comparing visual representations.
		  • Comparing each fraction to a benchmark.
		  • Comparing the two numerators when the fractions have the same denominator.
		  • Comparing the two denominators when the fractions have the same numerator.
			• Students use the wrong symbols ($<$, $>$, $=$).
			• Students order fractions the wrong way (ascending/descending).
			• Students think of the numbers (numerator and denominator) as two separate numbers.
			• Students inaccurately place fractions on the number line.
			• Students cannot properly represent

		• Students can compare and order two given fractions by creating equivalent fractions. • Students can order a given set of fractions in ascending or descending order. • Students can place fractions in relative order on an open number line.	fractions visually leading to inaccurate comparison.

Problem Types

Procedural Problems

- Represent $\frac{5}{2}$ pictorially.
- Record the improper fraction for the given pictorial representation:

- Arrange the following fractions in ascending order:
  $\frac{4}{8}$ $\frac{1}{3}$ $\frac{4}{5}$ $\frac{3}{10}$
- Use <, >, or = to compare the following fractions:
  $\frac{2}{3} \bigcirc \frac{4}{6}$
- Express the following as an improper fraction:
  $2\frac{3}{5}$
- Find two equivalent fractions for:
  $\frac{3}{4}$

Words-as-Labels Problems

- Sammie ate $\frac{1}{5}$ of dinner while Danny ate $\frac{2}{4}$ of dinner. How much of the dinner wasn't eaten?
- David was assigned to supervise $\frac{13}{5}$ rooms at the airport. Marsha was assigned to supervise $2\frac{3}{5}$ rooms at the airport. Who supervised more rooms?
- Andy has been a farmer for many years and knows that an egg carton typically holds 12 eggs. One day, Andy had 17 eggs to take to the market. Would $1\frac{1}{2}$ cartons be enough to hold the eggs?
- Three friends decided to paint the fence around their old school. Luis painted $1\frac{2}{6}$ fences, Helen painted $1\frac{1}{2}$ fences, and Shelly painted $\frac{5}{6}$ fences. Arrange the three friends in ascending order based on how much they painted.
- Dougie remodelled $2\frac{3}{4}$ rooms in the hotel. Samantha remodelled $\frac{15}{4}$ rooms in the same hotel. Who remodelled more of the hotel?

Open-Ended Problems

- Place two proper fractions and two improper fractions onto an open number line.
- Demonstrate the equivalency between an improper fraction and mixed number.
- Which fraction doesn't belong?

    $\frac{3}{6}$ $\frac{13}{6}$ $\frac{3}{3}$ $2\frac{1}{6}$

- Represent a fraction that is much larger than 1.
- Represent a fraction that is much smaller than 1.
- Three fractions are much larger than another fraction. Arrange these four fractions in ascending order.
- You have a combination of proper fractions, improper fractions, and mixed numbers. Place these on an open number line.

Rich Tasks

- Mark, Sally, and Scott volunteered to clean rooms after the hotel closed. Each of the three said that they cleaned the most rooms. When the manager checked the rooms, he noticed that Scott and Sally were close in the number of rooms they each cleaned, but both cleaned a lot more rooms than Mark. Using fractions, mixed numbers, and visuals, represent how many rooms Mark, Sally, and Scott each cleaned.
- A group of six students were chosen to create posters for the school winter carnival. The group started working on the posters during art club after school. At the end of art club, many students were still in the middle of working on a poster. To check the progress of the students, the teacher asked students to represent how many posters they made based on the following criteria:
    - If a student made less than two posters, record their progress as a fraction (proper or improper).
    - If a student just completed two posters, please record it as the number 2.
    - If a student completed more than two posters, record their progress as a mixed number.

    The teacher recorded these responses onto the whiteboard and asked students to place them on an open number line. What do you notice?
- A student shared a whole number, some improper fractions, and a few mixed numbers with you. He challenged you to arrange the numbers in ascending order. What do you notice?
- The teacher records a variety of numbers onto the whiteboard. There is one whole number, a few improper fractions, and less than five mixed numbers. When you place these on a number line, you notice that many of the numbers appear to be at one end of it. What could the numbers have been and how would they appear on a number line?

Ill-Defined Problems

- A local restaurant is creating a new menu and would like to know what kind of foods are popular with children. They were hoping we could help by testing some foods with our class and letting them know the fraction of students that liked each food.

- Our grade has a lot of students with different after-school plans. To make a safety plan for our school, we have to determine the portion of students attending similar after-school plans. This then needs to be shared with the teachers so that they can identify the most frequent plans.

Teacher Moves

Questions:

- What does that fraction represent?
- What does the numerator mean? What does the denominator mean?
- What would be an example of a fraction that we can see in this class?
- What strategy can you use to compare two fractions?
- Why is the representation of a mixed number the same as the representation for its equivalent improper fraction?
- What were you thinking as you placed the fractions on the number line?

Next Steps:

- If students are having difficulty understanding the whole, encourage them to circle the whole shape so that they know what the denominator represents.
- If students are thinking of the numerator and denominator as two separate whole numbers, have them draw lines from each to the corresponding aspect in the picture.
- If students are having difficulty applying the < and > symbol, have them use the terminology (less than, greater than) first. Then, use the terminology and record the symbol below the words. Then, move to only using the symbol.
- If students are having difficulty understanding the terms ascending and descending, provide opportunities to connect the terms to the phrases, "from least to greatest" and "from greatest to least."
- If students are having difficulty placing a fraction on the number line, determine if it is due to not understanding the magnitude of the fraction, the relationship between fractions on the number line, or a spatial sense concern.

Number: Relate Numbers

Be sure to refer to your curriculum for grade-specific expectations

	Brief Overview	*Look Fors*	**Common Misconceptions**
Relate Fractions, Decimal Numbers, and Percent	<ul><li>Percent can be introduced when the connection between fractions and decimals is made.</li><li>Percent is a part-to-whole ratio that compares a number to 100. Percent</li></ul>	<ul><li>Students can represent a given percent concretely and pictorially.</li><li>Students can record the percent displayed in any given concrete or pictorial representation.</li></ul>	<ul><li>Students are unable to convert between the fractions, decimals, and percent.</li><li>Students have a misunderstanding of fractions, decimals, or percent.</li></ul>

Relate Fractions, Decimal Numbers, and Percent	means "out of 100" or "per 100." • Percent can always be written as a decimal or vice versa. • Base-ten blocks and hundredths grids provide models to help make the connection between fractions, decimals, and percent.	• Students can express a given percent as a fraction and a decimal. • Students can identify and describe percent from real-life contexts. • Students can convert between fractions, decimals, and percent.	

Problem Types

Procedural Problems

- Express the following as a percentage and fraction:
  0.64
- Express the following as a fraction and decimal:
  9%
- Express the following as a percentage and decimal:
  $\frac{2}{5}$
- Represent 70% pictorially.
- Complete the following table:

Decimals	Percent	Fraction
0.73	73%	$\frac{73}{100}$
	16%	
		$\frac{7}{100}$
0.3		

Words-as-Labels Problems

- After checking their quiz, two students decided to compare their score. Todd had $\frac{4}{5}$ of the quiz correct while Donnie had 75% of the quiz correct. Each person thought they did better than the other. Who answered more questions correctly? Explain your thinking.
- A student scored on $\frac{2}{5}$ of her shots. What percentage of shots were goals?
- The MVP of the school's baseball team had a batting average of 0.43. What would this be as a percentage?
- While at the winter carnival, one child asked the ticket master what the likelihood was of winning a prize while playing a game. The ticket master replied that for every 10 people that play, three people win. What would this be as a fraction and percentage?
- There is a 30% chance of showers this afternoon. What would this be as a decimal?

Open-Ended Problems

- What fraction can be easily converted to a decimal?
- What percent can be easily converted to a fraction?

- Where do you see percent outside of school?
- Would you rather represent a situation as a decimal, percent, or fraction? Why?
- What are some denominators that you prefer to use when converting fractions to decimals and percent?

Rich Tasks

- There needs to be 60 new floor tiles installed in your classroom. There will be a combination of different colors of tiles. The principal has asked that the following conditions be met when installing the tiles:
    - A small percentage be blue.
    - At least $\frac{2}{5}$ of the tiles be white.
    - Less than 0.3 of the tiles be grey.
  Record, in percent, decimals, and fractions, how many of each color you will use.
- You are chosen to be part of the debate team. You must choose a fraction and a percent that are not equivalent. To prove this inequality, you must use pictures, numbers, and words.
- You are asked to arrange a percent, fraction, and decimal in descending order. There is no equivalency amongst these three representations. How can you convince others in the class that you have ordered the three correctly?
- On your last Science quiz, you answered 80% of the questions correctly. How many questions could have been on the quiz and how many did you get correct? What fraction of the questions did you answer incorrectly.

Ill-Defined Problems

- Our school is promoting healthy living. To contribute to this campaign, we are asked to create a poster that shares some statistics around the following:
    - Whether students exercise regularly.
    - Whether students eat a balanced diet.
- To make use of our persuasive writing skills, our class was asked to make a brochure on the importance of attending school regularly. The use of percent and fractions are encouraged to support our argument.

Teacher Moves

Questions:

- What does that fraction represent?
- What does the percent represent?
- What does the decimal number represent?
- What strategy do you use to convert between fractions, percent, and decimals?
- How can you verify that your conversion was accurate?
- Do you find it easier to use one representation (fraction, percent, decimal number) than another?
- Where do we see fractions, percent, and decimals outside of school?

Next Steps:

- If students are having difficulty converting between percent, fractions, and decimals, check to see if they understand each individual representation. If they don't, focus on strengthening their understanding of the representations.
- If students are having difficulty converting between percent, fractions, and decimals, and they do understand each of the individual representations, provide students more opportunities to visually represent each during the conversion.

Number: Integers

Be sure to refer to your curriculum for grade-specific expectations

	Brief Overview	*Look Fors*	**Common Misconceptions**

Represent Integers	• **Integers** include zero, positive, and negative whole numbers.
	• Integers should be read properly:
	  • When reading negative integers, –5 is to be read as negative 5, not as minus 5.
	  • Positive integers do not always show the "+" symbol. If no symbol is shown, the integer is positive (0 is neither positive nor negative).
		• Students can place given integers on a number line.
		• Students can extend a given number line by adding numbers less than 0.
		• Students understand and can explain the pattern on each side of 0 on a number line.
		• Students can describe contexts in which integers are used.
			• Students are confused with the signs.
			• Students are unable to place a negative integer on a number line.
			• Students do not understand the meaning of "–" when in front of a number.
			• Students do not remember that numbers without a sign are positive.

Compare Integers	• Concrete and pictorial representations are encouraged as students compare and order integers. • It is important to use mathematical language (equal to, greater than, less than) when comparing numbers.	• Students can place integers in relative order on an open number line. • Students can compare two integers and explain their rationale. • Students can order given integers in ascending or descending order.	• Students use the wrong symbols (<, >, =). • Students order integers the wrong way (ascending/descending). • Students inaccurately place integers on the number line. • Students do not understand signs (+ and –) and how this impacts the comparison, such as –9 < –4 because 9 > 4.

Problem Types

Procedural Problems

- Place the following integers on a number line:
  −1, 5, −5, 3, 9, −8, 0, +4
- Arrange the following integers in ascending order:
  +8, −9, 0, 2, −2, −5, 3
- Use <, >, or = to compare the following integers:
  −9 ◯ −7
- True or false? Explain.
  0 > −7
- Arrange the following integers in descending order:
  −1, −8, −2, +9, −4, 5, 1

Words-as-Labels Problems

- You are at the bank and ask to see the balance of your account. You decide to make a deposit of $8. Represent this action as an integer (using the proper sign).
- Sally recorded the following temperatures:

Monday	Tuesday	Wednesday	Thursday	Friday
−7°C	−8°C	−3°C	0°C	−3°C

  Which is the warmest day? Which is the coldest day?
- See the golfers score card below:

Monday	Tuesday	Wednesday	Thursday	Friday
+2	0	−3	+1	−2

  Arrange the scores in descending order.
- A submarine is at a depth of 402 metres below sea level. If sea level is represented as 0, what is the depth of this submarine as an integer (using the proper sign)?
- During class, the teacher asks if −8 is greater than −7. Carla said it is not because −8 is further away from 0. Dougie said it is because 8 is bigger than 7. Who is correct? Explain your thinking.

Open-Ended Problems

- Where would you expect to see an integer outside of school?
- What would be an example of a negative integer?
- What situation could be represented by −4?
- What situation could be represented as +7?
- I have recorded three negative integers and two positive integers. What could I be monitoring?

Rich Tasks

- The teacher said that she placed five integers on an open number line. She will not show you her drawing, but she will describe it:
  - There are five integers recorded on an open number line.

- Three of the five integers are much closer to one side of the open number line than the other side.
- The remaining two integers are closer to the middle.

Draw the open number line and place the five integers accordingly.

- The yearbook committee's bank account started the year at a balance of 0. Throughout the year, there were numerous transactions. The number of negative transactions was close to the number of positive transactions. Would the current balance be negative or positive? Explain your thinking.
- The temperature last Saturday was 0°C. For the past seven days, the temperature fluctuated up and down. Record the temperature for each of the past seven days and indicate what the current temperature is now. Explain your thinking.
- You were worried about your dog's weight and decided to start monitoring it. On the first of the month, you identified his baseline weight as 0 kilograms. Your plan was to weigh the dog every week. The first few weeks you saw the weight go down each time, but for the last number of weeks the weight has been gradually increasing. What would be the overall change in his weight considering 0 kilograms was his baseline? Explain your thinking.

III-Defined Problems

- The community is preparing to have outdoor events for its youth. To be well informed, the community would like to have a record of the change in temperature over the past few weeks. They are asking if we could share this data in a way that highlights the changes in temperature.
- The population of our primary and elementary classes has been changing over the past few years. Our school administration is asking us to share how the population of these two grade divisions have changed from year-to-year over the past number of years. This information will assist them in planning their budget projections.

Teacher Moves

Questions:

- What does that integer represent?
- What would be an example of an integer that we can see outside of school?
- What strategy can you use to compare two integers?
- What were you thinking as you placed the integers on the number line?

Next Steps:

- If students are having difficulty understanding the meaning of the "−" sign, share instances of negative integers outside of school (temperature, above and below sea level, and financial transactions such as credit and debit).
- If students have difficulty comparing negative integers, focus on using a number line and discussing distance from zero. When an integer is negative, the further it is from zero the smaller it gets.
- If students are having difficulty applying the < and > symbol, have them use the terminology (less than, greater than) first. Then, use the terminology and record the symbol below the words. Then, move to only using the symbol.

- If students are having difficulty understanding the terms ascending and descending, provide opportunities to connect the terms to the phrases, "from least to greatest" and "from greatest to least."
- If students are having difficulty placing an integer on the number line, determine if it is due to not understanding the magnitude of the integer, the relationship between integers on the number line, or a spatial sense concern.

Number: Addition & Subtraction

Be sure to refer to your curriculum for grade-specific expectations

	Brief Overview	*Look Fors*	**Common Misconceptions**
Add and Subtract Whole Numbers (Solve)	<ul><li>Addition and subtraction involve:<ul><li>The ability to solve addition and subtraction problems.</li><li>The ability to add and subtract numbers efficiently.</li></ul></li><li>Addition and subtraction should be taught simultaneously so students see the relationship between the two operations.</li></ul>	<ul><li>Students can solve addition and subtraction expressions concretely, pictorially, and symbolically.</li><li>Students can solve addition and subtraction word problems reflective of the four problem structures.</li><li>Students can create a word problem for a given number sentence or solution.</li></ul>	<ul><li>Students are not sure when to add or subtract.</li><li>Students make incorrect calculations.</li><li>Students have difficulty regrouping.</li><li>Students are not aligning digits.</li></ul>
Add and Subtract Whole Numbers (Estimate)	<ul><li>Estimation is the determination of an approximate solution using "friendly numbers" (numbers that are easy to mentally manipulate).</li><li>Estimation is encouraged as it can be used to judge the reasonableness of work.</li><li>Encourage the use of mathematical language when estimating; for example, about, approximately, between, a little more than, a little less than, close, close to, and near.</li></ul>	<ul><li>Students can provide context for when estimation is used.</li><li>Students understand and can describe contexts in which overestimating is important.</li><li>Students can determine the approximate solution to a given problem not requiring an exact answer.</li><li>Students can estimate a sum and a difference using an appropriate strategy.</li><li>Students can select and explain an estimation strategy for a given problem.</li></ul>	<ul><li>Students are not making accurate estimates.</li><li>Students change their estimate after calculation.</li><li>Students confuse estimating with rounding.</li><li>Students cannot explain their thinking.</li></ul>

Add and Subtract Decimal Numbers (Solve)	• All properties and developed strategies for the addition and subtraction of whole numbers apply to decimals. • Addition and subtraction should be taught simultaneously so students see the relationship between the two operations.	• Students can solve addition and subtraction expressions concretely, pictorially, and symbolically. • Students can solve addition and subtraction word problems reflective of the four problem structures. • Students can create a word problem for a given number sentence or solution.	• Students are not sure when to add or subtract. • Students make incorrect calculations. • Students have difficulty regrouping. • Students have difficulty understanding decimals. • Students are not aligning decimals.
Add and Subtract Decimal Numbers (Estimate)	• Estimation is the determination of an approximate solution using "friendly numbers" (numbers that are easy to mentally manipulate). • Estimation is encouraged as it can be used to judge the reasonableness of work. • Encourage the use of mathematical language when estimating; for example, about, approximately, between, a little more than, a little less than, close, close to, and near.	• Students can provide context for when estimation is used. • Students can describe contexts in which overestimating is important. • Students can determine the approximate solution to a given problem not requiring an exact answer. • Students can estimate a sum and a difference using an appropriate strategy. • Students can select and explain an estimation strategy for a given problem. • Students can use estimation to correct errors of decimal point placements in sums and differences.	• Students are not making accurate estimates. • Students change their estimate after calculation. • Students confuse estimating with rounding. • Students cannot explain their thinking.

Problem Types

Procedural Problems

- Solve:
    5.847 − 4.75
- Solve:
    16 + 23.05
- Estimate:
    201 837 + 343 395
- Estimate:
    90 233 − 39 323
- Which estimate is more accurate for 35.4 + 4.98:
    40 or 85.0

Words-as-Labels Problems

- The hockey rink had set aside $144 485 for construction. The cost to replace the flooring for the entire restaurant was $38 582. How much money does the hockey rink have left?
- Jill and Timmy were given $3500 to purchase outdoor supplies for their school. They decided to buy 3 benches, 2 slides, and 2 swings. How much money do they have left?

Supplies	Price
Bench	$215
Slide	$560
Swings	$695
Picnic Table	$250

- Two students are training for a marathon. Sean ran 6.52 kilometers in one hour. Anna ran 6.78 kilometers in one hour. Which of the two runners travelled further in the one hour training block and how much further was it?
- Your friend owes you $15.38. He gives you a $20 bill. How much money do you need to give him back?
- Joe spent $8.25 for a taxi on Monday and $5.72 for a taxi on Tuesday. How much money did Joe spend on taxis during those two days?

Open-Ended Problems

- The sum of two decimal numbers is a whole number. What could the two decimal numbers be?
- The difference between two large numbers is a 3-digit whole number. What could the two whole numbers be?
- The sum of two 4-digit whole numbers is a 5-digit whole number. What could the two 4-digit numbers be?
- The sum of two decimal numbers is a whole number. What are the two decimal numbers?
- The estimated difference between two decimal numbers is 80. What could the two decimal numbers be?

Rich Tasks

- You were asked to estimate the amount of money donated to the school food drive. You notice that there was a lot of money donated by the following groups: community council, families, staff, and students. How much money was donated by each of the four groups and what is the estimated total amount of money raised by the school food drive?
- The yearbook committee was interested in determining the price to charge students for the yearbook. They noticed that the cost of making the yearbook went up by a little bit compared to last year. As such, the committee decided to increase the price of the yearbook a little. What was the cost and price of the yearbook last year, and how does that compare to the cost and price of it this year?

- A group of students entered a scavenger hunt. The rules of the scavenger hunt are:
    - Teams are made up of a small number of students.
    - Teams need to successfully complete a stage before moving on to the next.
    - The distance each team travels (measured in meters) is used to determine the winner.

  Four teams entered a marathon. The total distance of each team was greater than 10 000 meters. What are the distances of each team and what is the difference between the team that placed first and the team that placed last?
- Over the course of a year, you keep track of how much money you spend on eating out at restaurants. You notice that you typically eat out a few times a month. About how much money do you spend a year at restaurants?

Ill-Defined Problems

- Our class has been challenged to create the breakfast menu for an upcoming week of school. As part of this challenge, we must decide on the menu and determine the cost of ingredients.
- We can finally go on a field trip. Where should we go and what will it take to get there?

Teacher Moves

Questions:

- How did you decide whether to add or subtract?
- How did you know that your response was accurate?
- What was your estimation strategy?
- What is the problem asking of you?
- Do you find it more difficult to add and subtract decimal numbers than whole numbers?

Next Steps:

- If students are having difficulty deciding whether to add or subtract, have them read the problem and think of it as a whole. Do not encourage key words as this is a misleading approach.
- If students are having difficulty recognizing the reasonableness of their response, have them reread the problem once they complete it to see if their response aligns with the other numbers.
- Encourage students to estimate a solution before calculating one. This estimate can be used as a way to self-monitor their work during the calculation.
- If students are having difficulty adding and subtracting decimal numbers, check to see if it is because they are struggling to understand decimals or if it is the process of adding and subtracting.
- If students are having difficulty aligning digits when adding or subtracting, offer grid paper.

Number: Multiplication & Division

Be sure to refer to your curriculum for grade-specific expectations

	Brief Overview	Look Fors	Common Misconceptions
Multiply and Divide Whole Numbers (Solve)	• Multiplication and division involve: • The ability to solve multiplication and division word problems. • Multiplication and division should be taught simultaneously so students see the relationship between the two operations.	• Students can multiply and divide concretely, pictorially, and symbolically. • Students can solve multiplication and division word problems. • Students can create a word problem for a given number sentence or solution.	• Students struggle with "groups of." • Students are unsure when to multiply or divide. • Students are unsure what to do with remainders. • Students have difficulty with regrouping. • Students have inaccurate multiplication/ division facts.
Multiply and Divide Whole Numbers (Estimate)	• Estimation is the determination of an approximate solution using "friendly numbers" (numbers that are easy to mentally manipulate). • Estimation is encouraged as it can be used to judge the reasonableness of work. • Encourage the use of mathematical language when estimating; for example, **about, approximately, between, a little more than, a little less than, close, close to,** and **near.**	• Students can provide context for when estimation is used. • Students can determine the approximate solution to a given problem not requiring an exact answer. • Students can select and explain an estimation strategy for a given problem. • Students can predict products and quotients using estimation strategies.	• Students are not making accurate estimates. • Students change their estimate after calculation. • Students confuse estimating with rounding. • Students cannot explain their thinking.

Multiply and Divide Decimal Numbers (Solve)	• Multiplication and division of decimals involves:
	  • The ability to solve multiplication and division word problems.
	  • The ability to multiply (decimal number by one-digit whole number) and divide (decimal number by one-digit whole number) efficiently.
		• Students can multiply and divide concretely, pictorially, and symbolically.
		• Students can solve multiplication and division word problems.
		• Students can create a word problem for a given number sentence or solution.
			• Students struggle with 'groups of.'
			• Students are unsure when to multiply or divide.
			• Students are unsure what to do with remainders.
			• Students have difficulty with regrouping.
			• Students have inaccurate multiplication/ division facts.

Multiply and Divide Decimal Numbers (Solve)	• The decimal point in a **product** and **quotient** must be determined using estimation skills, not a rule for simply counting decimal places.		• Students have difficulty working with decimals.
Multiply and Divide Decimal Numbers (Estimate)	• Estimation is the determination of an approximate solution using "friendly numbers" (numbers that are easy to mentally manipulate). • Estimation is encouraged as it can be used to judge the reasonableness of work. • Encourage the use of mathematical language when estimating; for example, **about, approximately, between, a little more than, a little less than, close, close to,** and **near**.	• Students can predict products and quotients of decimals using estimation strategies. • Students can place the decimal point in a product and quotient using front-end estimation. • Students can use estimation to correct errors of decimal point placement in a given product or quotient.	• Students are not making accurate estimates. • Students change their estimate after calculation. • Students confuse estimating with rounding. • Students have difficulty understanding decimals. • Students cannot explain their thinking.
Mental Math: Fact Learning	• Instant recall of basic facts is a building block for mental computation. • Quick recall of facts is 3 seconds or less.	• Students can select from various fact-learning strategies to find the most effective and efficient strategy. • Students can mentally process the facts in their mind in 3 seconds or less. • Students can explain their thinking.	• Students need to count on their fingers. • Students have difficulty recalling division facts (especially if multiplication facts aren't mastered).

Problem Types

Procedural Problems

- Solve:

  25.84×6
- Solve:

  45×28
- Solve:

  $16.53 \div 2$
- Estimate:

  0.8476×9
- Estimate:

  $74.384 \div 5$

- Which estimate is more accurate for 63.431 ÷ 3?
  2 or 20
- Without paper and pencil, solve:
  7×8
- Without paper and pencil, solve:
  $42 \div 6$

Words-as-Labels Problems

- Milk at school costs $0.75. If there are eight students in your class who each order one milk per day, how much would it cost your class each day for milk?
- It takes about 8 g of dough to make one cupcake. Marsha checks the label on the package and finds she has 143.6 g of dough. About how many cupcakes can Marsha make?
- Mary is building a bookcase and she needs to have 28.4 m of lumber to complete the project. Each piece of lumber is 4 m long. About how many pieces of lumber will she need to complete her project?
- Terri decided to buy a sled that costs $84.65. If she saves $9.25 each week for nine weeks, will Terri have enough money to buy the sled?
- Dana wants to buy two new video games. Together the cost for both games, including taxes, will be $195. Dana charges $14 per hour when babysitting. If Dana works for 13 hours, will she have enough money to buy the two video games?

Open-Ended Problems

- The product of two whole numbers is a 3-digit number. What are the two numbers and the product?
- The product of a whole number and decimal number is between 80 and 100. What could the whole number and decimal number be?
- The quotient is a 4-digit whole number. What could the dividend and divisor be?
- How does knowing what 5×8 equals help with solving 7×8?
- Two numbers were divided and the answer is between 20 and 25. What could the two numbers be?

Rich Tasks

- Meadowvale Elementary is a school with a population slightly under 100 students. To raise money for a field trip, the school decided to sell cookbooks. For each cookbook sold, the school would receive a small profit. If most of the students sell a cookbook, about how much money would the school raise?
- The public speaking club at school decided to have members present a collection. Each member in the club brought in their collection of either hockey cards or stamps. How many items were shared during the presentation?
- A large amusement park decided to divide its attractions into sections. The park managers wanted to have about the same number of people in each section. There were a lot of people scheduled to attend the park on opening day. How many people were assigned to each section of the park?
- The head coaches and assistant coaches of the school soccer team decided to treat the players to a pizza party. When the coaches received the bill for

the food, they decided to share it equally. How much did each coach have to pay?

Ill-Defined Problems

- We need to decide on a craft project for the school that all students can contribute to. By doing the craft as a school, we will need multiple people to bring each of the necessary materials. When you sign up for a material to bring, please indicate how much of the item you will bring. What could the project be and what amount will we have for each material?
- The librarian just purchased new fiction and non-fiction books at the school's book fair. They need help determining how to fairly distribute the books throughout all the elementary classes.

Teacher Moves

Questions:

- How did you decide whether to multiply or divide?
- How did you know that your response was accurate?
- What was your estimation strategy?
- What is the problem asking of you?
- Do you find it more difficult to multiply and divide decimal numbers than whole numbers?
- What mental math strategy did you use to solve the problem?

Next Steps:

- If students are having difficulty deciding whether to multiply or divide, have them read the problem and think of it as a whole. Do not encourage key words as this is a misleading approach.
- If students are having difficulty recognizing the reasonableness of their response, have them reread the problem once they complete it to see if their response aligns with the other numbers.
- If students are having difficulty applying mental math strategies, take inventory of what strategies they have mastered and then focus on supporting them knowing when to apply such strategies.
- Encourage students to estimate a solution before calculating one. This estimate can be used as a way to self-monitor their work during the calculation.
- If students are having difficulty multiplying and dividing decimal numbers, check to see if it is because they are struggling to understand decimals or if it is the process of multiplying and dividing.
- If students are having difficulty aligning digits when multiplying or dividing, offer grid paper.

Algebra: Solve Equations

Be sure to refer to your curriculum for grade-specific expectations

	Brief Overview	*Look Fors*	**Common Misconceptions**
Solve Equations with Variables	• An equation is a mathematical statement that includes an equal sign. The equal sign tells us that the quantity on the left is equal to the quantity on the right. • A symbol and/or variable is used to represent an unknown number in an equation.	• Students can solve a given equation with a single variable. • Students can express a given pictorial or concrete representation of an equation in symbolic form. • Students can express a given problem as an equation where the unknown is represented by a letter variable. • Students can create a problem for a given equation with one unknown.	• Students do not understand that the "=" symbol means equivalence/balance. • Students are unable to isolate the unknown variable. • Students confuse the variable "x" with multiplication sign.

Problem Types

Procedural Problems

Be mindful to move the unknown to be on the left and right sides of the equal sign. This will encourage the notion of equality and balance in equations.

- Find a number that makes each equation true:

$$12 = 2s + 4$$
$$3c = 7 + 5$$
$$5d = 22 - 7$$
$$18 \div 2 = 3m$$
$$4n + 3 = 19$$
$$40 = 8v$$
$$15 + j = 21$$
$$v = 3 \times 9$$
$$24 \div 4 = b$$
$$f + 4 = 8 + 9$$

Words-as-Labels Problems

- There were forty frisbees left on the playground at the end of recess. Eight staff members went out at the end of recess to do a playground check. When they saw how many frisbees were left on the playground, they decided they would each pick up the same amount. Write an equation that represents this context and solve.
- There were students playing tag at little recess and 4 more joined them. Then, at big recess, a group of 8 students and another group of 9 students joined those who were playing at little recess. Those who were playing at little recess formed one team and those who joined at big recess formed another team. Both teams were equal in numbers. How many children were first playing tag at little recess? Write an equation that represents this context and solve.

- The soccer team wanted cupcakes. Three players decided to take nine cupcakes to practice so that each player would have one. Write an equation that represents this context and solve.
- The school library had four boxes of graphic novels. The librarian found some more boxes in the storage room. Now there are seven boxes of graphic novels. How many boxes did the librarian find in the storage room? Write an equation that represents this context and solve.
- Four students brought some balloons to the party. While at the party, they found three more balloons. Now there are nineteen balloons. How many balloons did each friend take to the party? Write an equation that represents this context and solve.

Open-Ended Problems

- Create an equation in which the unknown number is small.
- Create an equation in which the unknown number is large.
- Create a word problem for an equation with an unknown number of 8.
- Create an equation that has both an addition and multiplication symbol.
- Create an equation that has a multiplication symbol on one side of the equal sign and a division symbol on the other side of the equal sign.

Rich Tasks

- A group of hockey players showed up to play a game of hockey. There were less than 10 people on one team. The other team had more players but decided to bench some players so that the two teams would be even. Write an equation for this scenario using a n to represent the number of players that were benched. Solve the equation.
- Mya and her friend Jackie each brought the same number of treats to book club. There were 18 treats in total. How many treats did each girl take? Write an equation for this scenario using a t to represent the number of treats that each girl took. Solve the equation.
- Five boxes of binders arrived at the school. You realize once you take all the binders out of the boxes, you will have to send three back so that there are the same number of binders as the staff of 22. How many binders are in each box? Write an equation for this scenario using a b to represent the number of binders in each box. Solve the equation.
- Two students created an equation with an unknown number (represented by m). When talking about their equations, both students shared that m represented the number 7. The two students assumed that their equations had to be the same. Is this true? Explain your thinking.

Ill-Defined Problems

Ill-defined problems are not typically applied to this particular key concept. However, students may engage in solving equations with variables as they work through ill-defined problems for other key concepts.

Teacher Moves

Questions:

- What does the <u>symbol representing unknown number</u> mean in this equation?
- What is the = symbol representing in this equation?

Next Steps:

- If students cannot identify the unknown number, first check to see if they understand the meaning of the = symbol (equivalence/balance).
- If students cannot identify the unknown, use blocks, an opaque bag (for the unknown number or blocks), and a balance scale. This concrete representation will assist students in understanding equations.

Spatial Sense: Measurement

Be sure to refer to your curriculum for grade-specific expectations

	Brief Overview	*Look Fors*	**Common Misconceptions**
Find the Perimeter, Area, and Volume	• **Perimeter** is the distance around a shape (measured in units). • **Area** is the amount of surface a space covers (measured in square units). • **Volume** is the amount of space an object occupies (measured in cubic units).	• Students can find the perimeter of a polygon. • Students can construct a polygon for a given perimeter. • Students can find the area of any rectangle. • Students can construct a rectangle for a given area. • Students can find the volume of rectangular prisms. • Students can construct a rectangular prism for a given volume.	• Students confuse perimeter, area, and/ or volume. • Students use inaccurate measurements. • Students make inaccurate calculations.

Problem Types

Procedural Problems

- Find the area.

23 m

3 m

- Find the perimeter.

- Find the volume.

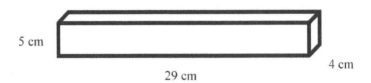

- Construct a polygon with a perimeter of 48 cm.
- Construct a rectangle with an area of 24 cm².
- Construct a rectangular prism with a volume of 36 cm³.

Words-as-Labels Problems

- A local jazz band wanted the community to give them a small piece of land that could be used as a stage. The community gave the band a rectangular piece of land with a perimeter of 40 m and an area of 96 m². What could the length and width be of this rectangular shape be?
- A classroom at Greenvale Elementary has a total area of 72 m². The length of this classroom is 9 m. How wide is the classroom?
- To prepare for winter, a farmer has built a shed for his farming tools. The volume of the shed is 42 m³. What is the height of this shed?

- As a summer job, Sami painted two bulletin boards. One bulletin board was 10 meters by 14 meters, and the other bulletin board was 15 meters by 8 meters. Sami charged $4 for each 10 m². How much did she charge to paint the two bulletin boards?
- The community maintenance person needed to buy fencing for a dog park. The dimensions of the rectangular dog park are 18 m by 23 m. What is the perimeter of the park?
- Before moving locations, a team had to pack up all its supplies into a large crate. The only crates they could find had a volume of 12 m³. The length of this crate was 3 m and the height was 2 m. What is the width of the crate?
- Dominic needs to mail a package to his cousin. The box is 24 cm long, 15 cm wide, and 5 cm high. The shipper will not ship anything with a volume greater than 1850 cm³. Will the shipper allow Dominic to ship the package to his cousin?

Open-Ended Problems

- The perimeter of a polygon was 48 m. Draw a picture of the shape and label the lengths of the sides.
- The area of the stage is 108 m². What could the length and width of the stage be?
- The volume of a storage container is near 20 m³. What are possible dimensions of the storage container?
- The perimeter of a rectangle is slightly less than 40 m. The area of this same rectangle is a bit more than 85 m². Draw a rectangle, with the dimensions labeled, matching these parameters.
- Two rectangular prisms have the same volume but look different. What could the dimensions be of each rectangular prism?
- When I add 1 meter to the length of a rectangle, the perimeter increases by 2 meters. However, the area of this same rectangle increases by more than 2 meters. Why?

Rich Tasks

- A student told his teacher that there are four possible arrays for an area of 36 cm². Is the student correct? How do you know?
- A group of students are creating a mural for the entryway of a school. The only three parameters put in place by the teacher are: 1) the mural has to be reflective of school spirit; 2) the mural must be rectangular in shape; and, 3) the area must be between 120 and 200 square centimeters. What could the dimensions of the mural be?
- An artist made a picture for a greeting card. The picture had an area of 56 cm². What are possible dimensions of this picture?
- Students were given nametags for their lockers. These nametags are rectangular in shape and have an area of 36 cm². What could be the least possible perimeter of these nametags?
- After raising money through various fundraisers, the city zoo was able to construct a new space dedicated to marine life. One area of this new space was an aquarium for small fish. The volume of this aquarium is slightly more than 100 cm³. Draw a picture of this aquarium with the dimensions labeled.
- While building rectangular prisms in class, two students noticed something interesting. Although both of their prisms were long, the volume of the prisms were significantly different. What could the dimensions of each rectangular prism be?

Ill-Defined Problems

- We need to rethink how our classroom space is organized. We need an adequate amount of floor space to facilitate the activities that we typically engage in during the day. Consider the tasks that are important to our learning and determine how to best plan and organize the space.
- Let's consider getting fish for our classroom. To do this properly, we must think about what we need to have a pet in our classroom and where it will be stored. What type of aquarium should be purchased for our choice of fish?

Teacher Moves

Questions:

- How did you decide whether to find the perimeter, area, or volume?
- What does perimeter mean?
- What does area mean?
- What does volume mean?
- Do you find it easier to find the perimeter, area, or volume? Why?
- Do you find it more difficult to find the perimeter, area, or volume? Why?

Next Steps:

- If students are having difficulty calculating the perimeter, area, or volume, determine whether it is due to not understanding the concepts or due to calculation errors. If it is not understanding perimeter, area, or volume, take time to focus on the foundational aspects that are vague. If it is operational struggles, provide guided practice on addition, subtraction, multiplication, or division.
- If students are consistently mixing up perimeter, area, and volume, encourage them to paraphrase the problems they are assigned and compare it to the meanings of perimeter, area, and volume. Use this process in determining which concept to apply to the problem.
- If students are having difficulty determining perimeter, area, or volume, encourage them to make a mark on the sides they have measured or included in the formula so that they don't forget to include it in the measurement and/or so that they don't double count a side.

Spatial Sense: Geometry

Be sure to refer to your curriculum for grade-specific expectations

	Brief Overview	*Look Fors*	**Common Misconceptions**
Measure Angles	• An **angle** is the space between two rays or line segments that are joined at a common point. • Angles are measured in degrees using a protractor.	• Students can identify angles found in the environment. • Students can classify a given set of angles (e.g., acute, right, obtuse, straight, and reflex). • Students can measure angles using a protractor. • Students can draw and label a specified angle. • Students can sketch angles for a given measurement. • Students can estimate the measure of an angle.	• Students are unable to accurately estimate angles. • Students cannot accurately use a protractor when measuring and/or constructing angles.

Problem Types

Procedural Problems

- Measure the following angle:

- Classify the following angle:

- Construct a 135° angle.
- Estimate the following angle:

- Sketch a 25° angle.

Words-as-Labels Problems

- A carpenter was working on designing a ramp that would allow wheels to be rolled from top to bottom. She decided to make this ramp an acute angle. Draw an example of what the ramp could look like.
- While watching an analog clock, you notice that 3:00 looks like an angle. Draw and classify this angle.
- Sammy measured an angle correctly and determined it was 125°. Her classmate, however, was confident it was 55°. What mistake might the classmate have made?
- While brainstorming how steep to make the toboggan hill for the winter carnival, the maintenance person deliberated between 20° and 75°. Which measurement do you think would be best? Draw the chosen angle and explain your thinking.

Open-Ended Problems

- Draw an angle for any measurement.
- Draw an angle that some would find difficult to measure.
- Sketch an angle that may not be challenging to classify.
- Draw an angle that may be easy to estimate.
- Draw two angles that look different but have the same measurement. Explain.

Rich Tasks

- As part of a scavenger hunt, you must find a few examples in the environment of different types of angles. What examples did you find for each angle type?

- You and a classmate are disagreeing about the measure and classification of an angle found at school. You insist it is an acute angle while your classmate insists it is a different type of angle. What type of angle could your classmate be insisting it is? How can both of you be confident in your responses?
- As part of an art project, you must create a picture that consists of numerous different types of angles. What will your picture look like?
- You make a shape that is mostly consisting of one type of angle. You decide to adjust this shape by adding in an angle that you have seldomly used. What is your original and revised picture?

Ill-Defined Problems

- As part of the winter carnival, our school has decided to take students sledding. We want to find the best place to sled with safety and speed being two of our main considerations. What are we looking for in terms of a hill?
- Our school soccer team is practicing shooting drills. The coach is wanting to know what angle is best if the players want to hit the corners of the net.

Teacher Moves

Questions:

- How did you determine the measure of the angle?
- How did you construct the angle?
- Do you find some types of angles easier to measure than others? Why?
- Do you find some types of angles easier to construct than others? Why?
- Do you find some types of angles easier to estimate than others? Why?
- How do you judge the reasonableness of a measurement for an angle?

Next Steps:

- If students are having difficulty measuring and constructing angles, determine whether it is a conceptual issue of angles or whether it is inaccurately using the protractor.
- If students are having difficulty classifying angles, determine whether it is due to not understanding how to measure angles or whether it is due to not knowing the classification of angles.

Data: Data Management

Be sure to refer to your curriculum for grade-specific expectations

	Brief Overview	*Look Fors*	**Common Misconceptions**
Collect, Record, Organize, and Analyze Data Using Graphs	• Graphs provide a great deal of information. • There are numerous types of graphs and some graphs are better at displaying collected data than others.	• Students can rationalize why they selected one type of graph over another. • Students can collect and graph data. • Students can interpret a graph.	• Students create unclear survey questions. • Students are unable to construct an appropriate graph. • Students have difficulty analyzing graphs.

Problem Types

Procedural Problems

- What type of graph would be best to show a pet's growth over a period of months?
- What type of graph would be best to show a parent's and children's favorite hobby?
- What type of graph would be best to show favorite ice cream flavours?
- What type of graph would be best to show the number of points a hockey team scored in the last seven games?
- Will the data in the following table require a series of points or a line graph?

Tree Growth	
2010	30 cm
2012	42 cm
2014	55 cm
2016	68 cm
2018	79 cm
2020	93 cm

Words-as-Labels Problems

- The school wants to make a graph that shows the favorite seasons of staff and students. After asking all staff and students, the data is as follows:

	Number of Students	Number of Staff
Winter	13	2
Spring	8	3
Summer	9	6
Fall	10	8

Draw a graph to represent this data.

- A group of retired people were asked about their favorite hobby. How many people were asked? What hobby was selected by nine retired people as being their favorite?

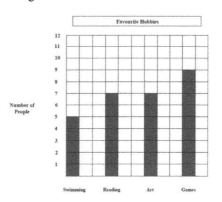

- A basketball coach kept track of how many points the center scored in each of the 12 games played at provincials in May. Which date in May did the center score the most points? How many points did the center score at the provincials in May?

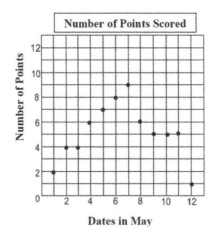

- Nancy is the school secretary. She's kept track of the number of students who signed up for yearbook each year since 2015. This is the data:

Year	2015	2016	2017	2018	2019	2020	2021	2022	2023
Number of Members	13	13	15	16	18	14	15	19	22

Create a type of graph that will best display this information. Be sure to include all the parts that are important for any graph.
- Scotty plans to use a line graph to describe his stamp collection. He wants to show how many stamps he has from each continent. Explain to him why a line graph is not an appropriate choice.

Open-Ended Problems

- What question could you write if you were interested in making a series of point graphs?
- Create a line graph that answers a question about you.
- Create a double bar graph based on your classmates.
- What questions could you ask someone to check if they understood the following graph?

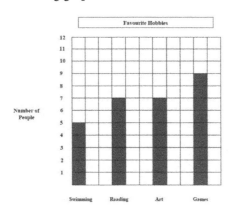

- Two double bar graphs could look very different even when displaying the same data. You may use sketches to demonstrate how this is a possibility.

Rich Tasks

- Your class is asked to create a graph outlining the total rainfall throughout a rainy day. Create this graph and think of three questions you could ask people to determine if they understand the data displayed in the graph.
- Some of the students in class are having a difficult time understanding the difference between continuous data and discrete data. You decide to create two graphs to explain the two types of data. One graph represents continuous data while the other graph represents discrete data. What are some of the questions you could provide during comparison?
- When analyzing a graph, you quickly notice that one category is more preferred by staff than students. What could such a graph look like?
- When analyzing a graph, you come to the realization that the data could be displayed in a much more effective way had a different graph been used. Provide an example of this by representing data using two different types of graphs.

Ill-Defined Problems

- Our community is looking into after-school programs but wants to make sure that they are suitable for our youth. The community is asking for help in crafting a plan.
- The school decided to purchase books for the library. It is important to get a range of books to address the various reading preferences of students.

Teacher Moves

Questions:

- What are you collecting data on? What is your question? How are you organizing the data?
- How will you display the data?
- What is the data telling us?

Next Steps:

- If students are having difficulty recording and organizing data, offer them a graphic organizer to assist in the process. Over time, you may remove this graphic organizer if students are demonstrating progress.
- If students are forgetting aspects in constructing graphs, provide a checklist of steps so that they can apply them. Over time, you may remove this checklist if students are demonstrating progress.
- If students are having difficulty analyzing data, offer them literal questions. Once students can demonstrate success answering literal questions, move to more analytical questions. Model for students and encourage them to talk through their thinking as they answer questions.

Financial Literacy: Cost of Transactions

Be sure to refer to your curriculum for grade-specific expectations

	Brief Overview	*Look Fors*	**Common Misconceptions**
Estimate and Calculate Cost of Transactions	• Contextual opportunities to calculate money amounts (decimals to hundredths). • Estimating and calculating cash transactions requires place value, addition, subtraction, multiplication, and division.	• Students can estimate the cost of a transaction that includes multiple items. • Students can calculate the cost of a transaction that includes multiple items.	• Students make inaccurate calculations. • Students are not sure which operation to use.

Problem Types

Procedural Problems

• Calculate the cost if you purchase each of the following items:

Item	Cost (including tax)
Basketball	$43.28
Basketball Hoop	$249.99
Basketball Jerseys	$176.25

• Estimate the total cost of the following purchases:

Item	Cost (including tax)
Television	$729.07
Tablet	$487.87
Desk	$398.76
Printer	$104.31

• The cost of a meal is $11.95. What is the total cost if four meals are purchased?
• The cost of purchasing a car is $24 131.95. What is the cost for each person if two friends agree to share it equally?
• You purchase three items that cost $457.11 individually. Estimate the cost of the transaction.

Words-as-Labels Problems

• A hockey player needs to buy a new stick and helmet for the upcoming season. The price of the stick is $108.95 and the price of the helmet is $215.95. All prices include taxes. If the hockey player purchases both items, what is the total cost?

- A group of three friends want to purchase a swimming pool. The cost of the swimming pool is $758.40. If the friends agree to share the cost equally, how much will each person pay?
- Leanne and John were given $3250.00 to purchase outdoor supplies for their school. They decided to buy 6 benches, 2 garbage cans, and 1 shed. Estimate the cost of the transaction.

Supplies	Price
Bench	$315.00
Garbage Can	$60.95
Shed	$695.99
Picnic Table	$250.99

- Marsha and Juan had to purchase supplies for the concert. They decided to buy seven speakers, four microphones, two storage bins, and two floodlights. The table that follows indicates the price of a single item. Estimate the cost of the transaction.

Supplies	Price
Floodlight	$487.55
Storage Bin	$310.95
Microphone	$595.98
Speaker	$809.99

- The cashier said the customer owes $173.09 for four books. When the customer heard this, he said that he was being charged too much as the price of each book was $42.98. Is the customer correct that $173.09 is too much for the four books? Explain your thinking.

Open-Ended Problems

- The estimated cost of a transaction including multiple items is $500. What could the actual cost of each item be that would make sense for such an estimate?
- The cost of one item is a lot more than the cost of another item. What is the cost of each item, and what would the total cost of the transaction be?
- The cost of the transaction was a bit less than $1000. What items did you buy and how much was each item?
- Estimate the cost of purchasing three items from table below.

Supplies	Price
Lawnmower	$2315.98
Lawn Swing	$467.35
Gazebo	$1696.99
Barbeque	$1230.64

- The total cost of the transaction was a 4-digit whole number. The cost of the individual items were 3-digit whole numbers. What were the individual costs of each item?

- You purchased a few of the following items. The total cost was around $3,000. What items did you purchase?

Supplies	Price
Lawnmower	$2315.98
Lawn Swing	$467.35
Gazebo	$1696.99
Barbeque	$1230.64

- You are asked to think about two items that you would like to purchase. The cost of purchasing these two items would total a lot of money. What items would you purchase and what is the cost of each item?
- You are told that you need to purchase some items from the following table. You have a choice of purchasing different items or multiple of the same item. What items do you purchase and what is the estimated cost?

Supplies	Price
Lawnmower	$2315.98
Lawn Swing	$467.35
Gazebo	$1696.99
Barbeque	$1230.64

- You are given a flyer from a popular store. You know an approximate amount of money you want to spend. If prices include taxes, what items will you purchase? Explain your reasoning.

Ill-Defined Problems

- The community is having a craft fair in our school's gymnasium. Vendors pay a $25 fee for each table they set up. People wanting to attend the fair must pay a $2 admission fee at the door. The community organizers will need to pay a rental fee to use the school on Saturday. Community organizers are asking us to find out an approximate number of vendors and attendees to make an appropriate profit.
- Our class will have a bake sale with all profits going to a local food bank. Let's decide on the food that we will sell at the bake sale. We will then need to purchase ingredients. What should we charge for each item and what profit will we expect to make from the bake sale?

Teacher Moves

Questions:

- What are the values of coins and paper money?
- What money value are you representing?
- How did you decide whether to add or subtract?
- How did you know that your calculations were accurate?
- What strategy did you use to make your estimate?

Next Steps:

- If students are having difficulty with the values of coins and paper money, offer visuals that will assist them in learning and remembering the values.
- If students are misrepresenting a given money value, take note if it is an addition/subtraction issue or a misunderstanding of the values of coins and paper money.
- If students are consistently arriving at an incorrect response, encourage them to paraphrase the problems they are assigned. By paraphrasing, students will strengthen their understanding of the problem and have a more informed plan of action.
- If students are having difficulty calculating the cost of transactions, check to see if it is because they are struggling to understand money values and decimals, or if it is the process of adding, subtracting, multiplying, and dividing.
- If students are having difficulty estimating the cost of transactions, check to see if it is because they are struggling to understand money values and decimals, or if it is the estimation process.

6

Making It Work

I will start this final chapter the way I started the book: acknowledging the messiness in mathematics. And, it is because of this messiness that I've developed a workable, three-part framework. Whether it is curriculum, student learning needs, differentiation, assessment, next steps, or relevant content, mathematics instruction is complex. Teachers cannot work any harder than they already are. But they can work smarter. By assigning various problem types for key concepts and applying teacher moves that are effective, teachers can engage in a manageable practice that allows them to reach the instructional goals they set for students.

Crafting Your Own Problems

I am guessing that you have spent considerable time searching for problems to assign in class. Sometimes it can feel like you are looking for a needle in a haystack. And, regardless of the time spent, you have yet to see the positive impact on student learning that you were hoping for. Whether students finish the problems instantly, do not know where to begin, or question the relevancy of the problem, the problems you are assigning are not providing the mathematical experience that you intended. In fact, many of the problems you find may seem like filler for the math block instead of opportunities for engagement and learning.

I don't want teachers to have to spend countless hours searching for problems that do not meet their intended goals. Instead, I want teachers to recognize the various problem types and be able to craft their own—in a way that is not taxing.

Defined Problems

The starting point for crafting defined problems is math. It is the teacher who identifies a mathematical concept students will engage with, and the problem is the tool students use to practice it. There are four types of defined problems: procedural, words-as-labels, open-ended, and rich tasks.

Procedural Problems

Procedural problems can be thought of as traditional *drill* type problems. These problems are intended to provide students with receptive practice in applying a specific concept. Typically, students are asked to calculate, identify, order, find, and/or solve while working with procedural problems. When crafting these types of problems, simply identify the concept and provide a prompt that will elicit students in applying the concept.

Words-as-Labels Problems

Words-as-labels, often referred to as word problems or story problems, have context. Teachers first select a concept and then decide on a context for the problem. The teacher then must decide on how to present data within the problem: within the text, as visual, or in a table. Once this is determined, the teacher must decide whether to add extraneous information as a way to increase the complexity of the problem. Finally, the teacher must decide whether the problem is single or multi-step. Words-as-labels are closed-ended problems that typically have one solution. With this type of problem, students must read through the context, decide upon a concept to apply, and then apply the concept.

Open-ended Problems

Open-ended problems have a great degree of openness. Teachers first decide on a math concept to be explored, then they craft a problem, out-of-context, that will provide access to a wide range of student-learning needs. These problems are quite different from procedural problems. When crafting open-ended problems, many tend to focus on a backward planning approach. Once you have selected a concept to be explored, you then consider an answer to a question that addresses the concept. Then, share that answer (or a range related to the answer) and ask students what could lead to such a solution (or range of solutions).

Rich Tasks

Rich tasks provide opportunities for students to make meaning within a familiar context. Such problems are intended to generate student engagement and interest. Rich tasks have similarities with words-as-labels problems and open-ended problems. Like words-as-labels problems, rich tasks have context and the teacher must decide how data is presented (within the text, as visual, or in tables), whether to add extraneous information, and how many steps comprise the problem. The difference is that rich tasks have many possible solutions. Like open-ended problems, rich tasks provide a great deal of openness to students in terms of strategy selection and possible solutions.

Ill-Defined Problems

The starting point for crafting ill-defined problems is context. Students must decide on which concept to apply to solve the problem. Therefore, it is not the teacher who decides which mathematical concept will be focused on, but the student. There is much more openness in ill-defined problems than defined problems.

To craft an ill-defined problem, you should consider the following questions:

- What is important to your students?
- What are you students interested in learning about?

- What is happening in your classroom?
- What is happening in your school?
- What is happening in your community?

By considering the questions above, you will be able to identify ill-defined problems that matter to your students and, at the same time, promote an experience that is relevant and meaningful to them.

Putting It All Together

When starting to work with the three-part framework, I recommend beginning with the identification of key concepts. Identifying key concepts first will enable you to narrow your focus in a manageable way. Having a narrowed focus will remove some of the messiness in math and will allow you to prioritize those math concepts that have leverage on other concepts.

Moving towards the three-part framework may mean that the problems being offered in the classroom need to be broadened to include a range of problem types. However, there is still good in what is being done. When applying the framework to your classroom, consider the following:

- What kind of problems do you tend to assign in the classroom? Do you rely on one or two problem type(s) more than others? What part of student learning would you like to strengthen (application: procedural; context: words-as-labels problems or rich tasks; openness: open-ended problems; relevancy: ill-defined)?
- Which problem type you would like to add to your repertoire that addresses your instructional target? Do not feel the need to add all other problem types right away as that will be overwhelming.
- Consider another problem type to add to your instructional repertoire. Once again, base this decision on your instructional goal.
- Continue to add additional problem types until your toolbox of problems includes four types of defined problems as well as ill-defined problems. Once you are familiar with all problem types (defined problems and ill-defined problems), move on to the next step.
- Are you providing students with opportunities to engage with the problem types that you have in your repertoire?

The sequence above is meant to be reflective exercise. By taking time to consider where you are at in terms of your mathematics instruction, you can identify next steps that are meaningful and manageable. Small steps will lead to big results. Introduce one problem type to your instructional repertoire at a time instead of trying to do it all.

Before moving further, I want to comment on balancing the various problem types in the classroom. I am not intending there be a 50/50 balance between defined problems and ill-defined problems. Instead, you may see more of an 80/20 relationship between them. This relationship does not suggest that ill-defined problems are less valuable than defined problems, it simply reflects an appreciation that ill-defined problems are more time-consuming than defined problems. I have seen many teachers who were unfamiliar with ill-defined problems start by assigning one or two a month. After some time, they become more comfortable in working through ill-defined problems and began to offer more throughout the year.

Remember: give yourself time. We have been immersed in the messiness of mathematics for a while now and we need to give ourselves permission to take our time while navigating towards a less messy approach. The three-part framework will be a valuable method that you can use to help you out of the messiness. With it, you'll find that your students will be more engaged, independent, confident, and better able to recognize the relevancy of problems. They'll begin to think mathematically, rather than just performing mathematical procedures.

Appendices

Problem Solving Graphic Organizer 1

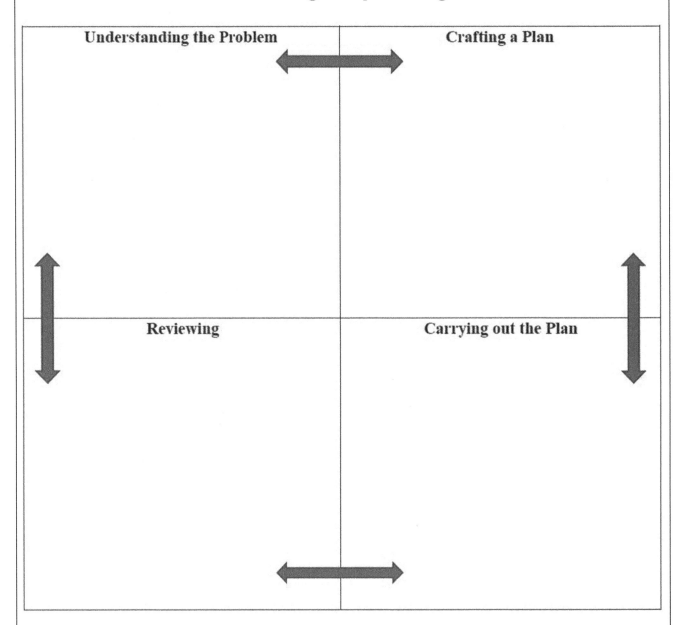

Understanding the Problem	Crafting a Plan
Reviewing	Carrying out the Plan

Source: Costello, D. (2022). *Mathematizing student thinking: Connecting problem solving to everyday life and building capable and confident math learners*. Pembroke Publishers Ltd.

Problem Solving Graphic Organizer 2

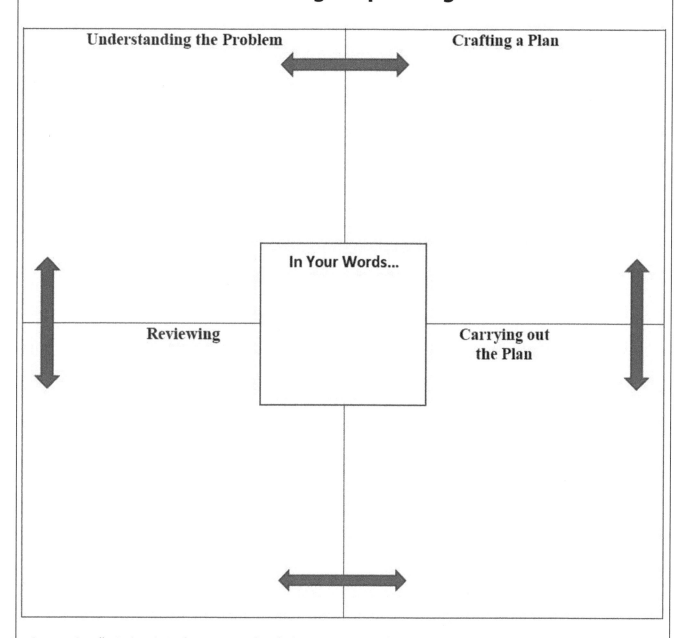

Source: Costello, D. (2022). *Mathematizing student thinking: Connecting problem solving to everyday life and building capable and confident math learners.* Pembroke Publishers Ltd.

Mathematical Modelling Graphic Organizer

The Process of Mathematical Modeling

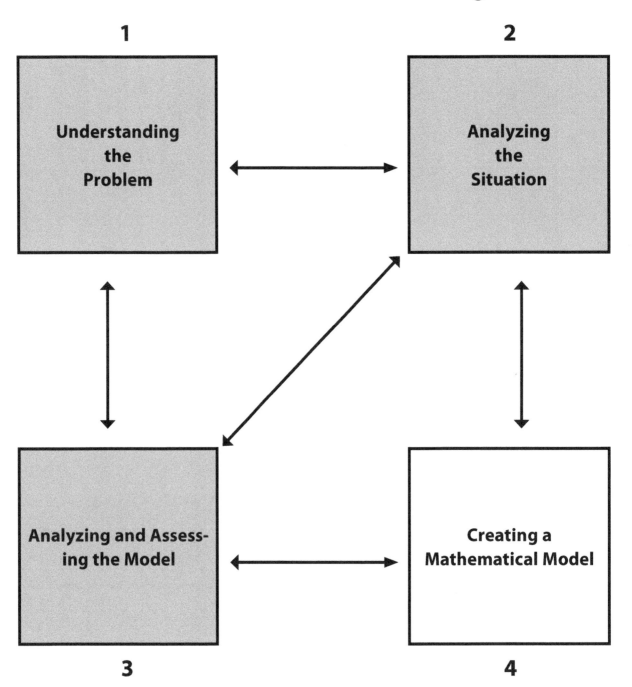

1

Understanding
the
Problem

2

Analyzing
the
Situation

3

Analyzing and Assess-
ing the Model

4

Creating a
Mathematical Model

Source: Costello, D. (2022). *Mathematizing student thinking: Connecting problem solving to everyday life and building capable and confident math learners*. Pembroke Publishers Ltd.

Key Concepts Checklist

Grade Level _____

Key Concept	Strand	*Look Fors*	Common Misconception(s)

Use this Key Concept Checklist to list all the key concepts for your grade level and the accompanying details (strand, *look fors*, and common misconceptions).

Pembroke Publishers ©2024 *Messing Around with Math* by David Costello ISBN 978-1-55138-366-8

Key Concept Plan

Grade Level _____

Key Concept	Strand	Problem Type				
		Defined Problems				Ill-Defined Problems
		Procedural	Words-as-Labels	Open-Ended	Rich Tasks	Ill-Defined

Use this Key Concept Plan to ensure that you are addressing defined problems and ill-defined problems for each key concept. It can be a great planning tool and reflective exercise.

Pembroke Publishers ©2024 *Messing Around with Math* by David Costello ISBN 978-1-55138-366-8

Key Concept Year Plan

Grade Level _____

Key Concept	Problem Type				
	Defined Problems				Ill-Defined Problems
	Procedural	Words-as-Labels	Open-Ended	Rich Tasks	Ill-Defined

Use this Key Concept Plan to plan out which month(s) you will address the various problem types for each key concept. It can be a great planning tool as it allows you to identify when problem types will be addressed for each key concept, whether it is one month or several months throughout the year.

Pembroke Publishers ©2024 *Messing Around with Math* by David Costello ISBN 978-1-55138-366-8

Glossary

area — is the amount of surface a space covers (measured in square units).

arrays — an arrangement of objects or pictures in columns and rows.

ascending — method of ordering items from smallest to biggest.

autonomy — being comfortable and confident in deciding on a plan and enacting it independent of support or direction from others.

consolidation block — the conclusion of the math lesson where the intent is to highlight the important ideas from the lesson, using student's work and thinking.

defined problems — problems that contain the information required to reach a solution. It is the job of students to use the given information to identify an effective strategy and to arrive at the solution.

denominator — the number below the line in a fraction, indicating the total number of parts in the whole or set.

descending — method of ordering items from biggest to smallest.

difference — the answer to a subtraction problem.

differentiation — tailoring instruction to meet the learning needs of students.

drill — repeated practice applying a concept.

endurance — outcomes and standards that focus on knowledge and skills that will be relevant throughout a student's lifetime.

equal groups — groups that contain the same number of items. It is often used in multiplicative situations.

essentiality — outcomes and standards that focus on the knowledge and skills necessary for students to succeed in the next grade level.

estimation — the approximation of an answer, whether it is numerical, concrete, or pictorial.

goal state — what is achieved and desired by the student. It is the preferred outcome of the problem.

ill-defined problems — problems that are missing one or more of the parameters that characterize defined problems. Ill-defined problems do not have a unique solution. What is important is that the response makes sense and that it addresses the question students encounter.

initial state — the state that students are presented with at the onset of the problem-solving process.

integers — a whole number that can be positive, negative, or zero.

key concepts — those curricular outcomes that have significant impact on student understanding and can be leveraged to assist students in learning other outcomes.

leverage — curriculum outcome(s) that focus on knowledge and skills used in multiple academic disciplines.

mathematical understanding — being able to recognize, apply, and understand mathematical concepts.

numerator — the number above the line in a fraction, indicating the number of parts identified.

obstacles — what happens between the initial state and the goal state. Obstacles would engage students in productive struggle as students would initially be unsure as to how to move from the initial state to the goal state.

open questions — see open-ended problems.

open-ended problems — problems are designed to allow for multiple solutions depending on the mathematical understanding students bring to the problem.

ordinal numbers — numbers that communicate the position or ranking of an item.

partitive — dividing a number into a particular number of groups.

percent — represents "out of 100" and is written using the symbol %.

perimeter — is the distance around a shape (measured in units).

problem types — various structures of math problems that have different learning goals associated with them.

procedural problems — problems are those where the strategy is already identified for students, and students must apply the steps accurately in order to reach the solution.

product — the answer to a multiplication problem.

quotative — dividing a number into groups of a particular amount.

quotient — the answer to a division problem.

rich tasks — the types of problems that provide students with an opportunity to make meaning within a context that is familiar to their lived experiences. Students are afforded the opportunity to select from a variety of approaches and representations as they work towards the solution, of which one or more can exist.

social-emotional learning skills — the development of self-awareness, self-control, and interpersonal skills, and the understanding of how these skills impact learning.

story problems — see words-as-labels problems.

subitizing — the ability to recognize the number of items without having to count.

sum — the answer to an addition problem.

teacher moves — high-yield instructional strategies. For this book, teacher questioning and identifying next steps are documented.

three-part framework — a framework that takes into consideration three parts of the learning process: curriculum (key concepts), instruction (problem types), and assessment and student learning (teacher moves).

volume — is the amount of space an object occupies (measured in cubic units).

word problems — see words-as-labels problems.

words-as-labels problems — problems can be thought of as simple, procedural word problems. These problems use words to provide context to a mathematical situation.

References

Ainsworth, L. (2003). *Power standards: Identifying the standards that matter the most*. Englewood, CO: Advanced Learning Press.

Costello, D. (2021). *Making math stick: Classroom strategies that support the long-term understanding of math concepts*. Markham, ON: Pembroke.

Costello, D. (2022). *Mathematizing student thinking: Connecting problem solving to everyday life and building capable and confident math learners*. Markham, ON: Pembroke.

English, L., Fox, J., & Watters, J. (2005). Problem posing and solving with mathematical modeling. *Teaching Children Mathematics, 12*, 156–63. Reston, Virginia: NCTM.

Greenwald, N. L. (2000). Learning from problems. *The Science Teacher, 67*(4), 28–32.

National Council of Teachers of Mathematics. (2014). *Principles to action: Ensuring mathematical success for all*. Reston, Virginia: NCTM.

Humphreys, C., & Parker, R. (2023). *Making number talks matter: Developing mathematical practices and deepening understanding, grades 3-10*. New York, NY: Routledge.

Krpan, C. M. (2013). *Math expressions: Developing student thinking and problem solving through communication*. Toronto, ON: Pearson.

Krpan, C. M. (2018). *Teaching math with meaning: Cultivating self-efficacy through learning competencies, Grades K-8*. Toronto, ON: Pearson.

McLennan, D. P. (2023). *Joyful Math: Invitations to play and explore in the early childhood classroom*. New York, NY: Routledge.

Newton, N., & Nuzzie, J. (2018). *Mathematizing your school: Creating a culture for math success*. New York, NY: Routledge.

Parker, R., & Humphreys, C. (2023). *Digging deeper: Making number talks matter even more, grades 3-10*. New York, NY: Routledge.

Small, M. (2013). *Making math meaningful to Canadian students, K-8*. Toronto, ON: Nelson Education.

Van de Walle, J. A., Karp, K. S., Bay-Williams, J. M., & McGarvey, L. M. (2017). *Elementary and middle school mathematics: Teaching developmentally* (5th Canadian ed.). Toronto, ON: Pearson.

Wedekind, K. O., & Thompson, C. H. (2023). *Hands down, speak out: Listening and talking across literacy and math.* New York, NY: Routledge.

Zager, T. J. (2023). *Becoming the math teacher you wish you'd had: Ideas and strategies from vibrant classrooms.* New York, NY: Routledge.

Index

Messing Around with Math

Ready-to-use problems that
engage students
in a better understanding
of key math concepts

DAVID COSTELLO

Pembroke Publishers Limited

© 2024 Pembroke Publishers
538 Hood Road
Markham, Ontario, Canada L3R 3K9
www.pembrokepublishers.com

Library and Archives Canada Cataloguing in Publication

Title: Messing around with math : ready-to-use problems that engage students in a better understanding of key math concepts / David Costello.

Names: Costello, David (Professional learning facilitator), author.

Description: Includes bibliographical references and index.

Identifiers: Canadiana (print) 20230581676 | Canadiana (ebook) 20230581749 | ISBN 9781551383668 (softcover) | ISBN 9781551389653 (PDF)

Subjects: LCSH: Mathematics—Study and teaching (Elementary)—Activity programs—Canada. | LCSH: Mathematics—Problems, exercises, etc.

Classification: LCC QA135.6 .C67 2024 | DDC 372.7/044—dc23

Editor: Renae Small, Alison Parker
Cover Design: John Zehethofer
Typesetting: Jay Tee Graphics Ltd.

Printed and bound in Canada
9 8 7 6 5 4 3 2 1